COME TO THE FEAST

Book 2

COME TO
THE FEAST

Book 2

All-age Services for
Ordinary Time based on the
Revised Common Lectionary

STUART THOMAS

Kevin
Mayhew

First published in 1998 by
KEVIN MAYHEW LTD
Rattlesden
Bury St Edmunds
Suffolk IP30 0SZ

0 1 2 3 4 5 6 7 8 9

ISBN 1 84003 257 X
Catalogue Number 1500222

Front cover: *Crowd IV* by Diana Ong,
reproduced by courtesy of SuperStock Ltd, London
Edited by Katherine Laidler
Typesetting by Louise Selfe
Printed and bound in Great Britain

CONTENTS

FOREWORD

I promised in the foreword to *Come to the Feast Book 1* that a second volume would be forthcoming. Having covered Advent and Christmastide, Lent and Eastertide, and several other important occasions, there were still 36 Sundays left to tackle. Most of this is 'Ordinary Time', Sundays described in the new lectionary as 'Propers', together with the two Sundays before Lent and the four leading up to Advent. It also includes Epiphanytide which is now kept as a festival season, with white as the liturgical colour, but starts us thinking about the life of Jesus, which we continue to study as we read consecutively through a Gospel each year.

Special Sundays should be highlights of the liturgical year, occasions we look forward to with anticipation, but that implies they stand out from the remaining 'ordinary' Sundays. It would be easy to dismiss these as less significant, but that would be wrong. The most important part of a child's diet as it grows up isn't the party food and special treats but the ordinary day-by-day nourishment it gains from less exciting fare. Similarly, in our maturing as Christians, the most important factor is regular reading, learning and study when there's no special focus. And, strange though it may seem, the spiritual 'highs' are more rewarding and fulfilling when they're backed up by this steady and consistent spiritual growth.

The Church of England's new lectionary (known to its friends as CLC2000, but essentially a slightly adapted version of the Revised Common Lectionary, now used by most of the mainstream churches) was introduced from Advent 1997 and is now its official lectionary. A significant proportion of parishes and other churches are already using it, but if yours is one that hasn't yet taken it on board, note that Year A starts from Advent 1998. In each of the three years a Gospel is read consecutively, starting usually before Lent and continuing right through from Trinity Sunday to Advent Sunday. The letters of the New Testament are also read consecutively, and for the Old Testament an option is given – either to read some of its books consecutively, or to read a passage which links in thematically with the day's Gospel reading.

The format of this book is identical to Book 1, in that it covers all three years of the lectionary. Each Sunday contains a confession and absolution, a responsive intercession, the readings for the Principal Service, some suggested hymns (both traditional and modern) and an outline all-age address for the Gospel reading. The non-thematic approach means that for many of the Sundays in Ordinary Time two or three outline all-age addresses are provided. All of the material is original, and most of it has been taken for a test drive before being set down on paper.

As in Book 1, the suggested hymns are from *Hymns Old & New*, New Anglican Edition. I've attempted as far as possible to fit them to one of the Gospel readings, and not to use any one hymn or song too often. Five traditional and five modern hymns are listed for each Sunday, but these lists are neither exhaustive nor definitive – I'm sure I'll have omitted some of your favourites!

The material is adaptable, and not intended to be a straitjacket. It should be tailored to local circumstance and used sensitively. Liturgical resources aren't an end in themselves, but exist only to enable people to engage in worship more fully and enter into a deeper relationship with our Lord Jesus Christ. This book, like its companion volume, is offered as a part of that process, so that our worship remains dynamic, engaging with and involving every member of the church community, so that every Sunday becomes a celebration of our faith in our crucified and risen Lord. As we learn more of him each week, we'll be fed and nourished in our spiritual life, and as we grow in him, so too we'll be strengthened to serve him better in this world.

STUART THOMAS

THE EPIPHANY TO ASH WEDNESDAY

The new lectionary treats Epiphanytide as a season, which, of course, it always was – Ordinary Time doesn't start until Candlemas. The liturgical colour is now white until 2nd February. But for most of us the celebration of the Christmas season is over by 6th January, with decorations put away in the loft, old wrapping paper ready for the recycling bin, and thank-you letters still to write. It's the start of a new school term, everyone's acclimatising to the new year, and it all feels rather lacking in festivity. However, Epiphanytide has its own distinct flavour, not allowing us to put Jesus aside but concentrating on the early part of his ministry in the four weeks before Candlemas, and thereafter on different aspects of his ministry until Ash Wednesday. From the Epiphany onwards our focus shifts from Jesus as a child to his adulthood and the three years of his ministry, before Lent and Holy Week take us into the final weeks of his life. We need to see the manger and the cross inextricably linked together.

First Sunday of Epiphany

The Baptism of Christ

It may seem strange that the Church of England hasn't recognised the Baptism of Christ as a festival until now, although the ASB did include it as the theme for the first Sunday of Epiphany. After all, it occupies a key place in Jesus' ministry and his own understanding of it. For a long time the Eastern Church used 6th January as the day on which they celebrated both Jesus' birth and Baptism, and it wasn't until the end of the fourth century that East and West settled on 25th December as the date for the former. Around the same time the Epiphany came to the Western Church from the East as the commemoration of Jesus' being revealed to the Magi, and more widely to the Gentiles. His Baptism thus moved to the first Sunday after the Epiphany where it remained in the Roman liturgical calendar. Since Epiphany marks the end of the Christmas season, the following Sunday provides the occasion to move on to the inauguration of Jesus' ministry, even though we return later, at Candlemas, for a final look back at his childhood and at the same time a look forward to his Passion.

It should be noted that when 6th January falls on a Sunday, it is also the first Sunday of Epiphany, and the Baptism of Jesus is celebrated on the following day. When 2nd February falls on a Sunday, the Presentation of Christ replaces the fourth Sunday of Epiphany.

The beginning of a new year is also an excellent point at which to emphasise the ministry of every member of the Church, and consider how each one's gifts can be utilised in the overall mission of the Church to fulfil its God-given vision. Some churches include a renewal of baptismal vows as part of their worship, but whether or not this is done, this is the ideal opportunity for the congregation as a whole, as well as its individual members, to reaffirm their commitment to following the way of Christ.

Hymns

TRADITIONAL

- *Come, Holy Ghost, our hearts inspire*
- *Lord of our life, and God of our salvation*
- *O Breath of Life, come sweeping through us*
- *O love, how deep, how broad, how high*
- *Thou, whose almighty word*

MODERN

- *I give you all the honour*
- *Jesus, Jesus, holy and anointed one*
- *Jesus shall take the highest honour*
- *Meekness and majesty*
- *O let the Son of God enfold you*

Readings

Year A Isaiah 42:1-9; Acts 10:34-43;
        Matthew 3:13-17
Year B Genesis 1:1-5; Acts 19:1-7; Mark 1:4-11
Year C Isaiah 43:1-7; Acts 8:14-17;
        Luke 3:15-17, 21-22

Confession

Lord Jesus Christ, beloved Son of God,
you submitted to the waters of Baptism
and lived in complete obedience
to the will of the Father.
We confess that we have not always been
submissive to your guidance
or obedient to your commands,
preferring instead to follow our own
selfish desires.
Forgive all our sins, we ask you,
and wash us clean.
By your Spirit make us fit for your service
and ready to obey your will,
that in our lives your name may be glorified.
Amen.

Absolution

God our Father,
who hears and receives all who come to him
in penitence and faith,
have mercy on you,
grant you pardon for all your sins,
strengthen you to walk with him in faith
and bring you the joys of eternal life,
through Jesus Christ our Lord. Amen.

Prayer

We bring to our heavenly Father
all our prayers and concerns,
and commit ourselves anew
to obeying and serving him as we say,
Lord we ask this in your name:
hear us and answer, we pray.

We bring to you the Church
throughout the world,
as it proclaims your saving love
and declares your eternal kingdom.
In unity of vision and purpose,
may all Christians work together
to obey Jesus' great commission,
making disciples and baptising people
of all nations and cultures
in the name of the Trinity.
Especially we pray for . . .
Make us firm in our faith
and joyful in our service.
Lord we ask this in your name:
hear us and answer, we pray.

We bring to you the nations of the world,
as they seek to uphold peace and righteousness
while fighting corruption and evil.
May your wisdom direct and rule
governments and leaders
as they decide matters of finance and trade,
justice and care, education and development.
Especially we pray for . . .
Make us strong in our convictions
and generous in our judgements.
Lord we ask this in your name:
hear us and answer, we pray.

We bring to you the needy and suffering
of the world,
as they struggle against the disadvantages
of poverty, starvation, homelessness
and exploitation.
May they know you alongside them
in their distress
and look to you to as the friend
who will never leave them.
Especially we pray for . . .
Make us aware of their needs
and alert to our responsibilities.
Lord we ask this in your name:
hear us and answer, we pray.

We bring to you those we know
who are sick in body or mind,
anxious, lonely or depressed.
May they trust you to bring them
comfort and healing,
and allow you to protect and guide them
through their times of difficulty.
Especially we pray for . . .
Make us sensitive in our caring
and loyal in our support.
Lord we ask this in your name:
hear us and answer, we pray.

We bring to you those who have passed over
into your eternal presence,
and those who are in the closing stages
of their earthly pilgrimage.
Especially we pray for . . .
May they know that your arms of love
are holding them,
and enter into the joy of your eternal presence.
Lord we ask this in your name:
hear us and answer, we pray.

We bring to you ourselves,
that throughout this week
your unfailing love will fill and inspire us,
and through us draw other people
into your kingdom of love,
for the sake of your Son, Jesus Christ. **Amen.**

All-age address

The Baptism of Jesus and the beginning of a new year offer an ideal opportunity to think about beginnings and starting out. Sociologists often stress the significance of how things are started and finished – even a new year. Witness the efforts that have been made to get the new millennium off on the right foot. While everyone accepts it's an arbitrary point in time, the start of a new year provides us with a useful time to review the past and put it behind us as we move forward on our life's journey. Jesus' Baptism was the ideal preparation, commissioning and act of commitment for the three years which followed, culminating in his Passion, death and Resurrection.

Athletics and sport provide a helpful illustration of the importance of getting a good start. If there's a member of the congregation who's a serious participant in some sporting activity, they may be willing to dress and equip themselves suitably to demonstrate the points being made – failing that, create some cartoon style pictures for the OHP, or take some from magazines or books. The example used here is athletics, but it should be clear how other sports can be used to make the same points.

1) No one will win their race or competition unless they're properly dressed and equipped. If you can persuade your volunteer to put on some inappropriate clothes over the top of their sporting gear, it will help reinforce the point that the correct equipment is a prerequisite to a good start. An athlete needs his running shoes and starting-blocks; a racing-driver needs a car filled with petrol; a skier has to have his skis waxed; a batsman must be wearing his pads and gloves ready to start his innings. Although Jesus was God's Son, it was important that the Holy Spirit descended on him to show that he was now fully prepared for his ministry over the next three years. We too need the Holy Spirit to equip us properly for whatever God calls us to do.

2) The right equipment is pretty useless without thorough training. At this point ask your volunteer to go through one or two fitness routines. Only with this regular training can an athlete be sure he's fit enough to compete with others. Jesus maintained his spiritual fitness by keeping up his prayer life and his relationship with his heavenly Father. Our Christian life depends on us doing the same.

3) Before he starts, an athlete also needs to know and obey the rules of his sport and accept the authority of the referee. He also needs to listen to the advice of his coach or another expert, so that his performance is always improving. Jesus, too, lived in submission to his heavenly Father, and although he was God's Son he willingly accepted the limitations that sharing our human life imposed. Our ministry can only be exercised in Jesus' name, on his authority,

and recognising our own human weakness and frailty. As we listen to his word, so we'll gradually become more like him.

4) Right at the outset, every athlete and sportsman needs to know what he's aiming for – the finishing line, the goal or a particular standard. Jesus was quite clear about where he was going and what he had to do. The course of his ministry certainly wasn't easy, and he knew that the pain of the cross lay ahead of him. But he also knew why he had to go through with it, and 'for the joy set before him he endured the pain of the cross' (Hebrews 12:2). We may not always be quite sure about the exact course of our journey of faith, but there's no need to doubt our ultimate destination. That will keep us going when things become difficult or tough.

SECOND SUNDAY OF EPIPHANY

Across all three years of the lectionary, the Gospel readings for this Sunday are taken from the first two chapters of John, covering the calling of the first disciples and the account of Jesus turning water into wine. Two different address outlines are provided, but the passages are complementary, focusing on how Jesus transforms not only the filthiest water in the house, used for footwashing, into the finest wine, but also on how his calling transforms the lives of a group of ordinary working men, who hear him and respond by leaving what they are doing to follow him.

Hymns

TRADITIONAL

- *All hail the power of Jesus' name*
- *Eternal ruler of the ceaseless round*
- *Father of Heaven, whose love profound*
- *God of grace and God of glory*
- *O for a closer walk with God*

MODERN

- *From the sun's rising*
- *Heaven shall not wait*
- *Lord Jesus Christ*
- *Will you come and follow me*
- *You are beautiful*

Readings

Year A   Isaiah 49:1-7; 1 Corinthians 1:1-9; John 1:29-42

Year B   1 Samuel 3:1-10; Revelation 5:1-10; John 1:43-51

Year C   Isaiah 62:1-5; 1 Corinthians 12:1-11; John 2:1-11

Confession

As we hear the voice of Jesus calling us,
we confess the sins
which have separated us from him, saying,
Lord, have mercy on us;
forgive us and strengthen us.

Lord Jesus, you called your disciples
to follow you in faith.
We too have heard your gracious call,
yet we confess that we have
not always heeded it.
Lord, have mercy on us;
forgive us and strengthen us.

Lord Jesus, you called your disciples
to listen to your teaching and learn your ways.
We too have heard your message of love,
yet we confess that we have often not acted on it.
Lord, have mercy on us;
forgive us and strengthen us.

Lord Jesus, you called your disciples
to stay with you,
however hard the circumstances.
We too have heard your call to faithfulness,
yet we confess that we have
sometimes preferred
to take the easier path.
Lord, have mercy on us;
forgive us and strengthen us.

Lord Jesus, we are truly sorry
that we have not always followed you willingly,
listened to you carefully
or stayed with you loyally.
Strengthen us by your Spirit,
that we may be faithful disciples of you,
our Master and Friend. **Amen.**

Absolution

God our merciful Father,
who forgives all who respond
to his loving call to repentance,
have mercy on you,
pardon you for all you have done wrong,
and grant you forgiveness for the past,
strength to live for him in the present,
and, in the world to come, eternal life.
Amen.

Prayer

We pray to Jesus Christ,
our Saviour and Friend,
listening for his gentle voice
and laying before him our concerns and needs,
saying, Lord, in the stillness of our hearts,
may we hear you speak.

Lord Jesus,
you call all Christian people
to live together in unity
and show your love in the world.
We pray for your Church
as it worships you and serves you,
both where there is peace and prosperity,
and where war and violence dominate.
Especially we think of . . .
May we live out our oneness in you
and work together to bring
your peace and justice
to this needy world.
Lord, in the stillness of our hearts,
may we hear you speak.

Lord Jesus,
you call the nations of the world
to deal with one another fairly and with justice.
We pray for everyone in a position
of authority or influence,
most of all in places where fear, conflict
and exploitation overshadow people's lives.
Especially we think of . . .
May we see how we can show
your love and care
to those who endure injustice and,
or who have been marginalised by society.
Lord, in the stillness of our hearts,
may we hear you speak.

Lord Jesus,
you invite those who are suffering
and burdened with care
to come to you and find rest.
We pray for those known to us
who are going through times
of difficulty and darkness,
whether in illness or bereavement,
anxiety or insecurity.
Especially we think of . . .
Lord, in the stillness of our hearts,
may we hear you speak.

Lord Jesus,
you call us to follow you throughout our lives,
not only in church but also in our relationships
with family, friends and neighbours,
in our daily work and our life in the world.
We pray that we may know your presence
throughout each day,
in times of activity and moments of rest,
so that in every situation
we may respond in faith to your prompting.
Lord, in the stillness of our hearts,
may we hear you speak,
listen to what you say,
and follow your leading,
for the sake of your kingdom. Amen.

All-age address 1

The idea that someone can be called by God to a particular task or ministry isn't encountered so much today. Perhaps we've become too used to shortlist interviews and IQ tests, or maybe it's now much easier to move jobs if we're not satisfied with our present employment, but somehow God's calling doesn't seem to play much part in career decisions. Unfortunately, the misunderstanding has grown that God's calling is only for those he wants in full-time ministry, that he isn't able to use human agencies to achieve his will. Jesus' calling of the disciples wasn't hampered by such misconceptions. When they heard his voice they followed at once, in part because they had little to hold them back, but most of all because he was utterly compelling.

This address makes use of the common experience of advertising slogans and campaigns, with a message aimed at persuading the consumer to part with his cash. Preparation involves selecting half a dozen or so fairly large advertisements (from a magazine, colour supplement, or even the endless fliers which drop through the letter-box or fall out of magazines) and pasting them on to a suitable piece of card. As far as possible choose those with a universal appeal, rather than ones for children's' book clubs or stair-lifts! The aim is to demonstrate that God's call is quite different from the blandishments of the media, not manipulative or ambiguous but direct and clear. Invite members of the congregation to give their own interpretation of the advertisement's message and whether or not they think its claims and presentation are honest.

1) Advertisements tend to appeal to our selfish instincts – something for a food product will illustrate this well. For example, there's nothing inherently wrong with a rather expensive brand of chocolate, but its appeal may well be more to our sense of self-indulgence than to our taste buds. After all, we're not going to buy a product which we don't believe will fulfil our needs and make us feel good. Jesus didn't appeal to his disciples' need for personal satisfaction, and God's call is never accompanied by a guarantee of permanent happiness and fulfilment. In fact, he made it quite clear that the Christian life is often difficult and demanding; but it offers a far deeper and more lasting sense of spiritual fulfilment rather than a 'quick fix' which wears off in no time.

2) Advertisements sometimes give the false impression that if only we'd buy a certain item our lives will be changed for ever. Here, a slogan for a household product or appliance should help reinforce the point. An electric drill is a great asset when making holes in a wall, and a microwave oven speeds up cooking times considerably, but neither are of the slightest use for washing clothes or playing CDs! God's call never exaggerates or distorts, and it applies to every part of our lives – it can truthfully claim to be life-transforming in every way!

3) It shouldn't be too hard to find an advertisement with a misleading message – something which costs 'only £ . . .' with other costs hidden in tiny print elsewhere, for example. God never misleads us. His call may be challenging or demanding, and will certainly have a cost, but we'll never feel 'conned' or disappointed if we respond to it.

4) By definition, advertisements try to push us into buying a particular product or service, investing our money in a certain account, or taking a course of action we otherwise wouldn't have considered. They try to convince us that our lives will be improved, our social status enhanced, our time and money better used – almost any advertisement could be used to show this. When the disciples heard Jesus' call it was compelling, but there were no false promises, appeals to self, misleading information or subtle attempts to overcome possible resistance. He wants us to follow him of our own free will, in response to his love and grace, not through manipulation or coercion. Many have found that the way of Jesus is costly – there's no such thing as cheap grace – but the benefits and blessings far outweigh anything this life can offer, transforming our lives for ever.

All-age address 2

As with all of Jesus' miracles recorded by John, the changing of water into wine can be taken on a number of levels. It shows Jesus' care for the guests to enjoy the wedding party and for the host not to be embarrassed; it shows him relating to the everyday joys and sorrows of human life; it shows how he takes the dirtiest water and transforms it into the best wine ever tasted; the wine is a symbol of Jesus' life given for us on the Cross and reminds us that through his death we have eternal life.

The props for this address are very straightforward – a bottle of red wine and some black grapes (a couple of different varieties if available). Start off by talking about wine-tasting and how connoisseurs savour a mouthful of each wine. Invite some children up, apologising that their age prevents you from allowing them to taste wine and offering them a grape-testing as an alternative! As they eat one, ask whether it was sweet or sharp, juicy or fleshy – there'll probably be a range of reactions.

Now explain briefly the process of making wine. The grapes aren't harvested until they're sufficiently ripe, but when they've been gathered in they're pressed either mechanically or (more rarely now) by treading. You may like to reassure the congregation that the latter won't be attempted in church – however, if you are brave enough, make sure you have the materials to hand to avoid too much mess and clean the volunteer up! It takes a lot of grapes to make one bottle of wine, and even after the grape juice has been collected it takes a long time before it can be bottled and sold, as it may be blended first, and then left to ferment until it's reached its ideal state. Make the parallel that like the grapes we can't be used until we're ready. God wants us to 'blend' with other Christians, and the Christian life is a long process of maturing.

But it's also true that we've been spoiled by sin, as grapes might rot because of a disease. We need the transforming power of Jesus to turn us from the mess of our wrongdoing into the best we can possibly be for him. By his death he gives us a completely new life, just as the grapes have a 'new life' as wine, and as we live by faith so we become more mature, however slowly.

THIRD SUNDAY OF EPIPHANY

Last week's Gospel readings were all taken from John's Gospel. The account of him changing water into wine reappears, this time in Year B, while the account of the calling of the disciples in Year A is taken now from Matthew's Gospel. The Year C Gospel is also about the beginning of Jesus' ministry, Luke's account of him preaching in the synagogue at Nazareth, his home town. This is an event of great significance both in our and Jesus' own understanding of his ministry over the following three years, even if it wasn't the public relations director's ideal start. It also raises questions about how we measure 'success' in the context of Christian work, and how we deal with conflict and opposition. It may be useful to note that in most years this Sunday falls in the Week of Prayer for Christian Unity.

Hymns

TRADITIONAL

- *Dear Lord and Father of mankind*
- *Jesus calls us: o'er the tumult*
- *Lord of our life, and God of our salvation*
- *Put thou thy trust in God*
- *Thy kingdom come, O God*

MODERN

- *As the deer pants for the water*
- *God's Spirit is in my heart*
- *I love you, Lord*
- *Lord, we come to ask your healing*
- *When God Almighty came to earth*

Readings

Year A   Isaiah 9:1-4; 1 Corinthians 1:10-18; Matthew 4:12-23

Year B   Genesis 14:17-20; Revelation 19:6-10; John 2:1-11

Year C   Nehemiah 8:1-3, 5-6, 8-10; 1 Corinthians 12:12-31a; Luke 4:14-21

Confession

Heavenly Father,
you sent your Son
to announce good news to the poor,
to declare freedom for prisoners
and restore sight to the blind.
We are sorry that we have failed
to follow in his ways,
turning our eyes from those in need,
and not sharing with them
the good news of Jesus.
Have mercy on us, we pray,
forgive our self-concern
and narrowness of vision,
and pour your Spirit upon us,
that our lips may declare your truth
and our lives show forth your loving care,
to the glory of Jesus Christ our Lord.
Amen.

Absolution

Almighty God,
whose love extends even to those
who turn away from him,
have mercy on you,
pardon and deliver you from all your sins,
set your feet on the right path
and bring you to eternal life,
through his Son, our Lord Jesus Christ.
Amen.

Prayer

Following the example of Jesus,
we come to our heavenly Father
with our thanksgiving and prayers,
laying before him the needs of the world
and the concerns of our hearts, saying,
Compassionate Lord,
hear us as we pray.

Your Son came to the poor
and brought them good news
of salvation and hope.
We pray for all who endure
the poverty of homelessness, poor housing,
or lack of basic resources,
and for those whose minds and spirits

are impoverished because of
their circumstances.
May they come to hear and respond
to your good news,
recognising Jesus
who comes alongside them
in every situation.
Compassionate Lord,
hear us as we pray.

Your Son came to those in captivity
and brought them good news
of freedom and joy.
We pray for prisoners and their families,
and for those who are enslaved
to addictive habits or substances,
asking for your wisdom and strength
to be given to those who support
and minister to them.
May they recognise the good news of Jesus
and enter into the freedom he offers.
Compassionate Lord,
hear us as we pray.

Your Son came to those who were blind
and brought them out of darkness
by giving them sight.
We pray for those who are handicapped
in body or mind,
and for those blinded to the truth
by fear or apathy,
that your good news may heal
and bring them life in all its fullness.
May they experience your transforming,
redeeming love
and rejoice that though once they were blind
now they can see.
Compassionate Lord,
hear us as we pray.

Your Son came to bring release
to all who are oppressed,
whether through the exploitation of others
or circumstances beyond their control.
We pray for those burdened
by illness and physical weakness,
anxiety or stress, especially . . .
May they know your presence in all their trials
and see in you the good news of release
from all that weighs them down.
Compassionate Lord,
hear us as we pray.

You call your people
to proclaim your love to everyone,
regardless of human differences.
May we be faithful messengers
of your good news,
so that those in need
may be drawn to the welcoming arms
of Jesus Christ, your Son, our Saviour,
in whose name we offer these prayers.
Compassionate Lord,
**hear us as we pray
and keep us true to our calling. Amen.**

All-age address

Jesus certainly made an impression when he returned to Nazareth – people couldn't believe how the local carpenter's boy could suddenly preach with such authority and conviction. He had a clear understanding that the famous passage from Isaiah did more than shed light on what he was about to embark on. It not only foresaw the events now unfolding but could only achieve its true fulfilment in them. At his Baptism the Spirit publicly descended on Jesus, and as a result he could claim to have been anointed for the work he was now starting. This isn't the easiest of passages to explain in the context of all-age worship, but this address takes the underlying message of God's love and care to emphasise a vital aspect of Jesus' ministry.

Preparation is simple, involving four large pieces of card and a marker pen. It uses a simple acronym for CARE, and the cards can either be held up by children at the appropriate moment or attached to a board so that everyone can see. In addition, you could find a suitable symbol to display for each word, to reinforce the message.

1) *C is for Compassion* – quite literally 'feeling with'. A simple symbol of this could be a box of tissues, which we might use if we're feeling upset and can share with others in the same state. This goes deeper than feeling sorry for someone or giving them a bit of a hand. Jesus had a particular feeling for the poor and the vulnerable, those unable to help themselves, and occasionally it got him into hot water with the authorities. Their primary concern was the preservation of the status quo, and they seem to have had

little interest in the needy, although there were undoubtedly some who took this aspect of God's law seriously. Throughout his ministry Jesus took the side of the poor and the oppressed, as he shared their feelings and concern. Just as we know God is alongside us in our suffering and pain, so we are called to be alongside others, showing them his compassion.

2) *A is for Announcement.* A large newspaper or magazine headline or slogan would do for this. Usually news is announced. Sometimes it's bad news, such as the announcement of Princess Diana's death, but it might equally be good news, like the birth of a baby or a forthcoming marriage. Jesus came to announce God's good news of salvation and new life, and this was to be directed at the poor – not just those who've run out of money, but those for whom life is miserable and hopeless, and those who recognise their own need before God. Good news is only really good for those who want to hear it. News of a hundred new jobs at a local factory may please the government, economists or local politicians, but it could be the best news ever for people in the area without a job, because they need it most. The more we recognise our own sinfulness and weakness, the more we realise how good the good news of Jesus really is.

3) *R is for Release.* A length of chain is a potent symbol of captivity, especially if you tie someone up with it (if you do, make sure in advance that it's clean and safe!). In former times prisoners were often held in chains, a very uncomfortable position, but Jesus is far more than a prison reformer. Many people are imprisoned by circumstances or bad habits, even today. Drug addicts and alcoholics aren't able to stop themselves damaging their bodies; those who get involved in crime often can't find a way out of their way of living; poverty and homelessness always seem to be a prison with no way out. Others are unable to escape from hurtful or traumatic experiences in the past. Jesus came to release all of us from the power of sin and death, and open up a whole new life.

4) *E is for Encouragement.* For those who knew their need of God, Jesus came to bring encouragement. He proclaimed 'the year of the Lord's favour' for them, that God's blessing would be on them, that God was on their side. An important part of caring is providing encouragement for those in need, reassuring them of their value to God, giving them confidence to cope with their problems, and setting hope before them instead of despair. However bad the immediate circumstances may be, there's always our ultimate hope to hold on to. Jesus encourages us to look away from ourselves and towards God, so that we can see the problems of this life in perspective, and become more determined to bring his good news to others.

FOURTH SUNDAY OF EPIPHANY

Year B	Deuteronomy 18:15-20;
	Revelation 12:1-5a; Mark 1:21-28
Year C	Ezekiel 43:27-44:4;
	1 Corinthians 13:1-13; Luke 2:22-40

As we approach Candlemas, the readings are still very much connected with the outset of Jesus' ministry. The miracle at the wedding in Cana now moves to Year A, with two quite different Gospel readings for Years B and C. The former is the first of Jesus' miracles recorded by Mark – the healing in the synagogue of a man possessed by an evil spirit – while the latter is the Candlemas Gospel from St Luke, the story of the infant Jesus being brought to Simeon and Anna. This Sunday quite often falls very close to the Feast of the Presentation, and, given its importance as the liturgical turning point between Jesus' incarnation and passion, the new lectionary not only allows it to be transferred to the Fourth Sunday in Epiphany, but even recommends this if more people can thereby share in observing it. An all-age address is outlined for the passage from Mark, while an outline for the Year A Gospel can be found under the Second Sunday in Epiphany. A suggested all-age address for Candlemas, based on the Year C Gospel, is included in *Come to the Feast Book 1*.

Hymns

TRADITIONAL

- *Glorious things of thee are spoken*
- *Immortal, invisible, God only wise*
- *Jesu, lover of my soul*
- *O God of Bethel, by whose hand*
- *Thy hand, O God, has guided*

MODERN

- *Faithful vigil ended*
- *Give thanks with a grateful heart*
- *Great is the Lord and most worthy of praise*
- *I give you all the honour*
- *Ubi caritas*

Readings

| Year A | 1 Kings 17:8-16; 1 Corinthians 1:18-31; |
| | John 2:1-11 |

Confession

We cry to God our Father in weakness and sin,
Lord, have mercy;
save us and heal us.

We confess to you our pride and stubbornness,
asking you to soften our hearts.
Lord, have mercy;
save us and heal us.

We confess to you our waywardness
and self-will,
asking you to set us on the right path.
Lord, have mercy;
save us and heal us.

We confess to you our blindness
and narrow-mindedness,
asking you to open our eyes
and restore our vision.
Lord, have mercy;
save us and heal us.

We confess to you our fear and lack of trust,
asking you to strengthen our faith.
Lord, have mercy;
save us and heal us,
forgive all our wrongdoing,
and make us whole, we pray,
for the sake of your Son,
Jesus Christ our Lord. Amen.

Absolution

God, whose will is for all people to be whole,
have mercy on you
and grant you forgiveness for all your sins,
peace in your hearts and minds
and strength to live for him day by day,
through his Son Jesus Christ our Lord.
Amen.

Prayer

Committing ourselves to the way of Jesus,
we pray for strength to obey his teaching,
and follow his example
in our homes, our community,
our work and our world, saying,
Lord, help us to follow your way,
and fill us with your love.

Jesus, when you lived on earth
you made deaf people hear
and blind people see.
We ask you to be with all whose lives
are affected by physical or mental handicap,
and to give strength to those who care for them.
Help us to value everyone equally as you do,
and extend your love to them.
Lord, help us to follow your way,
and fill us with your love.

Jesus, you welcomed all
who came to you in faith,
and never turned away anyone in need.
We ask you to open our eyes to see
those in need around us –
the homeless, the vulnerable, the abused –
and to move our hearts
to put their interests above our own.
Lord, help us to follow your way,
and fill us with your love.

Jesus, you confronted the scheming
of wicked people
with your truth and goodness,
and spoke out against self-righteousness
and hypocrisy.
We ask you for courage to stand firm
against evil and wrongdoing,
and, by the way we live, to challenge
the selfishness and greed we see all around.
Lord, help us to follow your way,
and fill us with your love.

Jesus, you healed people
of all kinds of illnesses and conditions
and made them whole again.
We ask you to give comfort and healing
to all who are suffering,
whether in their bodies or their minds,
and to bring peace and joy
to those who are distressed or anxious.

We especially remember . . .
Lord, help us to follow your way,
and fill us with your love.

Jesus, you came to bring us life in all its fullness.
We ask you to heal us of all that would harm,
and make us whole by your Spirit,
that we may worship you joyfully
and serve you faithfully
in whatever we are called to do in your name.
Lord, help us to follow your way,
**and fill us with your love
so that it flows to everyone we meet
and draws them into your presence,
for the sake of your kingdom. Amen.**

All-age address

It would be possible to take the passage from Mark's Gospel as a straightforward account of a healing miracle, but Mark seems to play this aspect down. Significantly, it follows straight on from Jesus' Baptism and his calling of the disciples, the emphasis being more on the power and authority Jesus demonstrated in his ministry from the outset. Following a similar line, this address outline is essentially dramatic, focusing on the different elements of Jesus' ministry and requiring a number of volunteers. It's described here as a mime, acted out without words, but if your actors are up to it, you might prefer to construct a simple script – making sure that it won't take up too much time!

1) We see Jesus first as a teacher. If possible, dress up a volunteer as a teacher in gown and mortar-board, and provide them with a blackboard and chalk (or whiteboard and marker pen). One or two children could be pupils, who give the teacher a hard time, refusing to learn their times-tables or spellings. Before long the teacher has to stop teaching and tell them off, as they're learning nothing. Point out that Jesus' teaching was nothing like this. When he spoke, everyone listened attentively, not just because he was a great speaker and storyteller, but also because his words had power and authority. Jesus was altogether different from the teachers of the law, who

went on at great length but bored everyone to tears and carried no conviction. Even today his teaching has an impact on people far beyond any other teaching before or since. We listen to his words, not to gain more information or knowledge, but because they show us the love of our Father in heaven, and set us on the way to eternal life.

2) *Next we see him as healer*. Although this certainly wasn't unknown in those days, there's little doubt that Jesus' miracles were unprecedented, seen as evidence of his authority over diseases and the powers of evil. For this tableau a doctor is needed, with a stethoscope, white coat and any other suitable props. He also needs a patient to treat, with a leg injury perhaps, or a sore throat, who could leave with a prescription in his hand. Explain that when we visit the doctor we hope he can diagnose our problem and prescribe the necessary remedy, but we don't usually expect him to make us better on the spot. In this case Jesus healed the man there and then, and even did it on the Sabbath in the synagogue. Quite simply his compassion for the man was so great that he saw no need to delay making him whole again, even in front of a full congregation! Nor does he stop at putting right or masking a symptom, but instead goes to the root of the problem. The healing power of Jesus makes us whole as people, even if we still have to go to the surgery occasionally for medication.

3) *Finally we see Jesus as leader*. For this a soap-box, set up in front of a microphone, will be ideal for a politician – you could even hang up a poster saying, 'Vote for Jones'. After a few shouted slogans, say that we're well used to political figures telling us what's best for us and making all kinds of promises about what they'll do, though we don't always take them very seriously! Jesus' hearers were probably just as used to that from their religious leaders, who were also the government in those times. But Jesus was quite different. No one ever accused him of being 'all talk and no action'. He kept his promises and demonstrated a kind of authority they'd never seen before –

even the forces of evil obeyed him! Yet throughout his ministry Jesus made it clear that he wasn't acting off his own bat or furthering his own reputation; his authority came from his heavenly Father and everything he did came out of that relationship. The risen Jesus still draws people to the love of God our Father, and whatever we do in his name we also do on his authority. We may not become famous that way, but with God's strength we'll get done whatever he wants for his kingdom.

PROPER 1

Sunday between 3rd and 9th February inclusive
(if earlier than the Second Sunday before Lent)

The period of time between Candlemas and Ash Wednesday varies in length according to the date of Easter. Only very rarely, if Easter is exceptionally early, do no Sundays fall in it at all; very occasionally it will contain five Sundays, in those years when Easter Day comes nearer to the end of April. Usually there are two or three Sundays. The new lectionary gives the two Sundays immediately before Lent distinctive themes, and these take precedence over the first three Sundays in Ordinary Time, or 'Propers'. Proper 3 is used least, only in years where there are five Sundays before Ash Wednesday. Do remember that the new lectionary doesn't follow themes; during Ordinary Time in each of the three years it follows one of the synoptic gospels sequentially, starting on this Sunday – the suggested hymns also reflect the readings rather than a specific theme. Year A's passage from Matthew is a part of the Sermon on the Mount; in Year B we read Mark's account of Jesus both healing many people and praying alone; in Year C Luke describes the calling of the disciples, including a miraculous catch of fish. The outline address for the Second Sunday in Epiphany will fit this last reading, while two others are suggested for Years A and B.

Hymns

TRADITIONAL

- *Awake, awake: fling off the night*
- *Bright the vision that delighted*
- *Christ is the world's true light*
- *Immortal, invisible, God only wise*
- *We have a gospel to proclaim*

MODERN

- *A new commandment*
- *Fill your hearts with joy and gladness*
- *I, the Lord of sea and sky*
- *Inspired by love and anger*
- *Lord, the light of your love*

Readings

Year A   Isaiah 58:1-9a (9b-12);
         1 Corinthians 2:1-12 (13-16);
         Matthew 5:13-20
Year B   Isaiah 40:21-31; 1 Corinthians 9:16-23;
         Mark 1:29-39
Year C   Isaiah 6:1-8 (9-13);
         1 Corinthians 15:1-11; Luke 5:1-11

Confession

Father God,
we confess in sorrow our failure
to keep God's commandments,
or to live in love and peace with one another.
We are sorry for our waywardness,
and repent of our self-will.
In your great mercy forgive us, we pray,
and so make your light shine through our lives,
that others may see your love
and glory revealed,
and come with us to worship you,
through Christ our Saviour. Amen.

Absolution

God our Father,
whose mercy is unending
and whose love is without limit,
grant to you pardon for all your wrongdoing,
the assurance of sins forgiven,
and peace both here on earth
and in the life to come,
through Jesus Christ our Lord. Amen.

Prayer

Lord Jesus,
you are the Light of the World,
and those who follow you
will have the light of life.
Hear us as we pray now
for the Church and the world, saying,
Lord, the light of your love is shining;
dispel the darkness, we pray.

Lord Jesus,
the world is full of people who live
in the darkness of despair and misery.
We remember the millions

of homeless street-children,
the frail and elderly,
refugees displaced by civil war,
and those living in the midst of violence
in fear for their lives,
and especially . . .
Bless all who minister to them in your name
and seek to relieve their suffering.
Lord, the light of your love is shining;
dispel the darkness, we pray.

Lord Jesus,
there is darkness in high places,
where governments have been
corrupted by power
and the mass media rule people's lives.
We pray for those in positions of authority and influence,
who may be tempted to put ambition or greed
above their integrity and responsibility;
may your light guide them
in the paths of truth and righteousness.
Lord, the light of your love is shining;
dispel the darkness, we pray.

Lord Jesus,
there is darkness in many homes
and communities,
where people are in conflict
and the vulnerable are exploited
or left to fend for themselves.
We pray for families divided
by relationships breaking down,
children neglected or manipulated,
lives damaged by substance abuse,
neighbourhoods in fear of crime and violence;
may your light bring them warmth
and reassurance in their distress.
Lord, the light of your love is shining;
dispel the darkness, we pray.

Lord Jesus,
some of our friends and loved ones
are overshadowed by the darkness
of ill-health or bereavement.
We remember today by name . . .
May your light bring them
comfort in their suffering,
healing in body, mind and spirit,
and the hope of salvation.
Lord, the light of your love is shining;
dispel the darkness, we pray.

Lord Jesus,
we remember with gratitude and affection
those who have passed through
the darkness of death
and now rejoice in the light
of your eternal presence,
remembering especially . . .
May we follow their example
of faith and courage,
and one day share with them
the glories of heaven,
where there is no darkness,
only the light of your glory shining for ever.
Lord the light of your love is shining;
dispel the darkness, we pray,
for the sake of your kingdom. Amen.

All-age address 1

The Sermon on the Mount is arguably the best-known piece of teaching Jesus ever gave, combining great insight and profundity with a simplicity and accessibility which anyone could relate to. Jesus didn't use jargon or mindless clichés. Instead, he took illustrations from everyday life which were familiar to his hearers, and told stories. This address outline develops the pictures in this passage of Jesus' followers being salt and light. Only a small amount of preparation is required.

1) Bring out a salt cellar or grinder, and begin by asking one or two congregation members what they would use salt for. The most likely first answer is 'on chips'! Others may then mention vegetables, meat, or even eggs. At this point bring out a hard-boiled egg in an egg cup, saying, 'Here's one I prepared earlier', and ask who likes boiled eggs. You could invite one of those who does to come and taste this one, or if you prefer, try it yourself. When the egg has been cracked open, sprinkle a little salt on it and comment on what effect this has. When salt is well sprinkled it brings out the taste of the egg, but if it's all stuck together in one place, not only will it taste horrible, but you will probably start coughing and need a long drink – have a glass of water handy! Before it was associated with health problems, salt had a vital function in preserving meat, so

explain that Jesus wants those who follow him to do the same for their community and society, because if they don't, it'll start to go bad. Equally, if they all stick together they can't possibly bring out the good or prevent the bad.

2) Now produce a torch, and demonstrate some of its uses. A volunteer could shine it into a grubby corner or under a pew, for example, or use it to find their way into a dark area. It could be an aid for reading, or even act as a beacon. All these purposes show how Jesus wants his followers to be the light of the world. If his light is within us, it will shine out to others, showing up what needs to be cleaned up and put right; it will bring guidance in times of uncertainty; it will help us to see and do God's will; and it will be visible to everyone, drawing them to Jesus, the Light of the World.

Conclude by saying that the aim of the salt is not to be salty, but to preserve and to bring out the taste. Similarly, a torch is of use only when it shines on something else. We can only be used by God if we draw attention not to ourselves but to him.

All-age address 2

In the passage from Mark 1, we see two different aspects of Jesus. In the first part he's on the go all the time, healing first Peter's mother-in-law and then crowds of other people who'd come in all kinds of need. In fact, the pressure continues until well past bedtime. So the second part portrays him slipping away to a quiet place where he thought he could pray undisturbed. Eventually Peter finds him and they move on to other villages nearby to carry on with his ministry. This very simple outline uses two well-briefed volunteers to mime this contrast.

1) The first one is seated at a table or desk, on which there is a diary and telephone, together with plenty of scrap paper and a few pencils. He/she sits there scribbling away, answering the phone, getting up and going across the church and returning, leaving a pen where

they went. As the phone keeps ringing they get more frantic, paper falls on the floor, the pen can't be found . . . Quote the old proverb 'more haste, less speed', and say that while this person does a good job and means well, he's just too busy. He's not taking time to think about what he's doing so everything starts to go wrong. Christians can easily allow themselves to get too busy, feeling guilty if they're not doing something, but doing so much that none of it gets done well. Of course, there are times when all of us have more to do than time to do it in, but like Jesus we must recognise how important it is to stop and take time out with our heavenly Father.

2) Now bring on the second volunteer, dressed and equipped as a doctor. As he enters, the manager collapses in a heap on his desk, exhausted by his efforts. The doctor listens to his chest, takes his temperature and so on, and tells him he needs a good rest, at which point they can move across to a comfortable chair. He can't work effectively until he's sorted himself out. Say that if we just carry on doing things and never taking time for prayer or reflection, we'll end up doing nothing properly and becoming spiritually tired. When Jesus needed to spend time in quiet with his Father, he wasn't being idle, but getting the necessary rest and refreshment to continue with his ministry. We need to do this just as much as he did – a particularly useful point to bring out in the run-up to Lent.

PROPER 2

Sunday between 10th and 16th February inclusive
(if earlier than the Second Sunday before Lent)

The Gospel readings for this Sunday follow on from last week's, with Year A continuing the Sermon on the Mount and Jesus' interpretation of the law, Year B recounting the healing of a leper, while Year C looks at the 'Sermon on the Plain', Luke's summary of Jesus' teaching which parallels the Sermon on the Mount.

Hymns

TRADITIONAL

- *Be thou my vision*
- *Father, Lord of all creation*
- *Forth in thy name, O Lord, I go*
- *I know that my Redeemer lives*
- *Lord of our life, and God of our salvation*

MODERN

- *Bind us together*
- *Fill your hearts with joy and gladness*
- *Let there be love shared among us*
- *Make way, make way*
- *O Lord, all the world belongs to you*

Readings

Year A   Deuteronomy 30:15-20;
         1 Corinthians 3:1-9; Matthew 5:21-37
Year B   2 Kings 5:1-14; 1 Corinthians 9:24-27;
         Mark 1:40-45
Year C   Jeremiah 17:5-10;
         1 Corinthians 15:12-20; Luke 6:17-26

Confession

We come to kneel in repentance
before our heavenly Father as we say,
Lord have mercy on us;
pardon and deliver us, we pray.

We repent of the wrong we have done:
hurtful gestures, careless behaviour
and selfish acts.
Lord, have mercy on us;
pardon and deliver us, we pray.

We repent of the wrong we have spoken:
insensitive conversation, harsh criticism
and cynical comments.
Lord, have mercy on us;
pardon and deliver us, we pray.

We repent of wrong thoughts and attitudes:
ill-disguised resentment, unfair judgements
and self-centred desires.
Lord have mercy on us;
pardon and deliver us, we pray.
Take away our sin, purify our hearts,
and make us holy as you are holy,
through Christ our Lord. Amen.

Absolution

Almighty God,
whose mercy is without end,
grant you pardon and forgiveness
for all your sins,
wisdom to speak and act rightly,
and confidence in your eternal calling,
through Jesus Christ our Lord. Amen.

Prayer

Remembering Jesus' love
for the poor and vulnerable,
we bring our prayers for them
to our heavenly Father,
praying as he teaches us,
Your kingdom come,
your will be done.

Lord Jesus,
we pray for the poor and needy,
those who are marginalised
or forgotten by the rest of the world –
the homeless down-and-outs,
the street children, the underpaid workers
and refugees displaced from their homes.
Through the care and compassion
of your people
may they be reassured of their place
in your heart.
Your kingdom come,
your will be done.

Lord Jesus,
we pray for those who hunger and thirst
after righteousness –
aid-workers, carers of the elderly
or handicapped,
peacemakers and campaigners
for justice and peace.
Through their devotion and commitment
may your love be spread
throughout the world.
Your kingdom come,
your will be done.

Lord Jesus,
we pray for those who are persecuted
for their faith –
Christians who are imprisoned
or disadvantaged by the authorities
for challenging evil
and upholding what is right.
Through their boldness and courage
may your church be built up
and our own faith strengthened.
Your kingdom come,
your will be done.

Lord Jesus,
we pray for those who mourn or despair –
the bereaved and grieving,
the chronically and terminally sick,
the depressed and anxious,
the frail and infirm.
Especially we commend
to your healing grace . . .
Through their suffering
may they know the comfort
of your presence
and the joy of your salvation.
Your kingdom come,
your will be done.

Lord Jesus,
we pray for our own witness and service,
and ask that we will rejoice
even in tough times,
knowing that our reward is in heaven.
In our decisions and actions
may your kingdom come,
**your will be done,
for your name's sake. Amen.**

All-age address

A recent TV commercial, inviting recruits to the teaching profession, consisted of a number of well-known figures simply saying the name of their most inspiring teacher. All children are familiar with the role of teacher, and there will be very few adults who can't remember something of their schooldays, so this outline looks at Jesus as one of the most memorable and inspiring teachers of all time. Ideally a volunteer can be progressively dressed up and equipped as a schoolteacher to make the points visually, but it would be just as effective to use a cartoon drawing of one on an OHP slide, adding to it with each point made.

1) We expect a teacher to know his or her subject and to speak authoritatively about it – an academic gown or mortar board will do very well here. Jesus' authority came not from academic studies but from his heavenly Father, whom he listened to all the time and obeyed implicitly. Our sharing of the good news will be effective only if we too live in trust and obedience to God our Father.

2) Teachers sometimes have to correct inaccurate work or bad behaviour – a cane will provide cartoon-style amusement value, but, if you feel this conveys an unhelpful message, a detention book or similar will do just as well. Jesus also corrected people when they misunderstood God, and made it clear that wrong behaviour has to be dealt with.

3) Really good teachers inspire their pupils and bring out the best in them, enabling them to develop their full potential. The simplest illustration may be a blackboard and chalk, but a pile of erudite books will be satisfactory, provided you make the connection that depth of knowledge and enthusiastic communication are essential to good teaching. Explain how Jesus wanted all his hearers not only to understand the truth of what he was saying, but also to know it as a reality in their personal experience. Our heavenly Father isn't an academic obscurity but our Creator who loves us and wants us to enjoy life as he meant us to.

4) The best teachers make a difference to their pupils not just in the classroom but for the rest of their lives. Often our best subjects at school are those that were taught most enthusiastically. If possible, a couple of enthusiastic volunteer pupils doing homework or research can help make this point. Conclude by saying that as we learn from Jesus, he will change the course of our lives too, just as he did the disciples'. His teaching is easy to understand, practical and life-changing, and unlike a schoolteacher we can carry on learning from him throughout our lives.

PROPER 3

Sunday between 17th and 23rd February inclusive
(if earlier than the Second Sunday before Lent)

The readings for this Sunday will be among the least used in the entire lectionary, since they only appear when Easter falls so late that there are five Sundays between Candlemas and Ash Wednesday. The Gospel readings from Matthew and Luke in Years A and C continue with passages from the Sermons on the Mount and Plain respectively, while Year B takes Mark's account of the paralysed man lowered through the roof to be healed by Jesus.

Hymns

TRADITIONAL

- *Christ is made the sure foundation*
- *Dear Lord and Father of mankind*
- *Jesu, priceless treasure*
- *Praise to the Holiest*
- *The Lord is King! Lift up thy voice*

MODERN

- *Be still, for the presence of the Lord*
- *Brother, sister, let me serve you*
- *God forgave my sin in Jesus' name*
- *Jesus put this song into our hearts*
- *O Lord, all the world belongs to you*

Readings

Year A   Leviticus 19:1-2, 9-18;
          1 Corinthians 3:10-11, 16-23;
          Matthew 5:38-48
Year B   Isaiah 43:18-25; 2 Corinthians 1:18-22;
          Mark 2:1-12
Year C   Genesis 45:3-11, 15;
          1 Corinthians 15:35-38, 42-50;
          Luke 6:27-38

Confession

God of love,
your Son taught us that all your commandments
are summed up in the law of love.
We acknowledge that we have not loved you

with all our heart, soul, mind or strength,
nor our neighbours as ourselves.
We are sorry and ashamed,
and repent of the wrong we have done
and the good we have failed to do.
Have mercy on us, we pray,
cast out our sins,
and give us strength to obey you willingly
and courage to serve you joyfully,
for the sake of your Son,
our Saviour Jesus Christ. Amen.

Absolution

Almighty God,
source of all grace and mercy,
hear your cry of repentance,
pardon all your sin and wrongdoing,
and grant you the blessings of eternal life
both in this life and in the world to come,
through his Son, Jesus Christ our Lord.
Amen.

Prayer

We come to Jesus our Saviour,
casting all our burdens on him,
secure in the knowledge that he cares for us,
and saying,
Jesus, Master and Friend,
hear the prayer of our heart.

We bring our concerns for your Church
in every corner of the world,
for its preaching of the Gospel,
its care of the needy, and its unity.
May all your people set aside
differences of tradition and culture
to work together for your kingdom,
making your name known in every place,
and bringing your love into every situation.
In particular we pray for . . .
Jesus, Master and Friend,
hear the prayer of our heart.

We bring our concerns for the world we live in,
for its governments and political figures,
its mass media and communications systems,
its financial and commercial interests
and its many areas of intense suffering.
May all in leadership positions think wisely,

speak sensitively, and act compassionately
to promote justice and peace,
and counter corruption and evil.
Jesus, Master and Friend,
hear the prayer of our heart.

We bring our concerns for the sick and dying
and those who look after them,
for medical and nursing staff,
for carers and counsellors,
for rescue and emergency services,
and for the work of homes and hospices.
In particular we pray for . . .
May they experience your peace
and comfort in their suffering,
and feel your healing hand reaching out to them.
Jesus, Master and Friend,
hear the prayer of our heart.

We remember those who have died in faith,
and their friends and loved ones
who mourn them, especially . . .
May we follow in their steps
in our earthly pilgrimage,
so that one day we may also share with them
the joy of heaven.
Jesus, Master and Friend,
hear the prayer of our heart,
and guide us through this earthly journey
into eternal life,
through your risen Son,
Jesus Christ our Lord. Amen.

All-age address

This outline address is based on the passage from the Sermon on the Mount, though it could be used on other occasions too. The aim is to move away from the concept of the Christian faith as a set of regulations to adhere to or rules to keep, using instead Jesus' teaching to establish the 'rules' by which he wants us to live. A small amount of preparation is necessary to obtain suitable visual aids.

Begin by asking the congregation when they're required to obey certain rules. An early answer will almost certainly be 'when driving', while others might mention our obligations as citizens of our country, as employees of a particular organisation, or as students. From this it is easy enough to clarify that there are different kinds of rules and laws.

1) There are rules to keep us safe, for example on the roads. A copy of the Highway Code will exemplify this, as would a large copy of a road sign. If people disobey these there'll be a major accident.

2) There are rules to protect people and their property, which make burglary and violent behaviour, for example, serious offences. A copy of a legal document will reinforce this, or you could dress someone in a policeman's helmet to indicate enforcement of these rules.

3) There are rules to keep order, not least in school – if nobody kept them, there wouldn't be much learning going on! A detention book or cane will again make this point. They may be unpopular, but such rules are for the benefit of all who come under them.

4) There are rules to ensure that everyone is treated fairly, by employers, traders, authorities and so on. A salary slip could be produced at this point.

5) There are rules to maintain society as we want it – paying taxes and following procedures, for example, come under this heading. Continue to use the salary slip here, or bring out instructions for water usage or something similar.

These laws are good and necessary, but the law of Jesus is quite different, because it emphasises good behaviour rather than the consequences of bad behaviour. You couldn't make laws about it, let alone enforce it! In this passage Jesus mentions four rules which are part of his law of love:

1) Love your enemies – not *like* them, it should be added. Love isn't a problem when we find someone easy to get along with, but is altogether more demanding with those we find hard-going or downright awkward. As someone said, 'It's difficult to love God, because we haven't seen him, but far harder to love our neighbour because we have!' Jesus goes further than saying we're just to put up with them – he wants us to 'go the second mile' and put ourselves out for them.

2) Treat other people as you'd want them to treat you. Few people would disagree with the sentiment, but we all find it much harder to achieve in practice.

3) Do good without expecting a return. Our society is very short on generosity of spirit, or wallet, and often people will refuse to give anything if there isn't a possible pay-back. Jesus doesn't want us to think only of what we'll get out of acting generously, but to give freely as he does, without strings attached.

4) Be merciful to other people, because in so doing we're reflecting our heavenly Father's character. Our society and culture is often brutally harsh, unforgiving of failure and cynical about success. There seems to be little place for compassion or kindness, let alone unconditional giving. As followers of Jesus we're called not to be negative or judgemental, but forgiving and accepting (though explain that this isn't the same as being a doormat or tolerating wrong), sharing God's love without adding any small print.

SECOND SUNDAY BEFORE LENT

The Church of England's new lectionary makes very few alterations to the Revised Common Lectionary, and on this Sunday only it goes its own way, making this one of the very few Sundays in Ordinary Time to have a clear theme. Creation was originally the first theme in the Sundays before Christmas in the ASB, but, since these have now been replaced, it was considered important to retain this focus elsewhere during the year, and in a quite different way from Harvest. Even outside the Christian community many people are concerned about the world we live in and the way we treat (or maltreat) it, so this presents a great opportunity to address the message of the Gospel in a context few will fail to relate to. The Gospel reading for Year A continues with the Sermon on the Mount, Year C relates how Jesus calmed a storm, while Year B returns to the Prologue to John's Gospel.

Hymns

TRADITIONAL

- *Angel-voices ever singing*
- *Come, Holy Ghost, our hearts inspire*
- *Eternal Father, strong to save*
- *Give to our God immortal praise*
- *I cannot tell why he whom angels worship*

MODERN

- *Christ triumphant*
- *Dance and sing, all the earth*
- *Inspired by love and anger*
- *Moses, I know you're the man*
- *Seek ye first the kingdom of God*

Readings

Year A Genesis 1:1-2:3; Romans 8:18-25; Matthew 6:25-34
Year B Proverbs 8:1, 22-31; Colossians 1:15-20; John 1:1-14
Year C Genesis 2:4b-9, 15-25; Revelation 4; Luke 8:22-25

Confession

Father God, Maker of all,
you created the heavens and the earth
and everything in them,
and saw that they were very good.
You put your life in each one of us
and made us the high point of your creation,
appointing us as the earth's stewards.
Yet we have failed to keep your command,
using the world to fulfil our own selfish desires,
instead of caring for it
and sharing its resources
for the benefit of all people.
We are sorry and ashamed,
and repent of our lack of concern,
our unwillingness to change,
and our self-centredness.
Forgive us, we pray,
and in your mercy restore us to yourself,
that here we may live for your eternal kingdom,
and, in the life to come,
may enjoy your presence for ever,
through Jesus Christ our Lord. Amen.

Absolution

Almighty God,
the Creator and Redeemer of all,
have mercy on you,
pardon and deliver you
from all selfishness and sin,
make you worthy servants of his kingdom,
and bring you at last to eternal life,
through Christ our Lord. Amen.

Prayer

We pray to God,
the Creator and Sustainer of all life,
for our world and its needs, saying,
Lord of life,
in your mercy, hear us.

God has entrusted us
with the care of a world
both beautiful and fragile,
yet human greed has damaged and scarred it.
We pray for those whose livelihood is threatened
by the forces of exploitation and materialism,
and for those who struggle to ensure

that we act as wise stewards
of the resources of creation.
Lord of life,
in your mercy, hear us.

God has commanded all people
to treat one another with respect and care,
loving as he loves us,
yet conflict and violence abound
throughout the world.
We pray for all who live in fear and insecurity,
or under the threat of ill-treatment,
and for the peacemakers who seek
to bring an end to warfare and suffering.
Lord of life,
in your mercy, hear us.

God has commanded his Church to live in unity,
working together for the sake of his kingdom,
yet often our differences and disputes
have overshadowed our calling.
We pray for all Christian leaders,
teachers and evangelists,
that they may show us the way
to overcome the barriers of the past
and join together united in worship and witness.
Lord of life,
in your mercy, hear us.

God has commanded us
to live as members of one body,
differing in activity yet one in purpose.
We rejoice with those who rejoice, especially . . .
and share the pain and hurt
of those who suffer through illness
of body or mind,
depression or anxiety,
loneliness or bereavement,
in particular . . .
Lord of life,
in your mercy, hear us.

God has promised
to all who live by faith in him in this world
a place in heaven with his saints
who have gone before us.
We remember with gratitude . . .
Lord of life,
in your mercy, hear us,
receive our prayers ,
and bring us with them to your eternal home,
through Christ our Lord. Amen.

All-age address

People are probably far more aware today of their environment than ever before, although sadly we fall far short of God's ideal in our stewardship of it. Children are especially conscious of ecological issues, even at a quite early stage of their education, while most adults can now be persuaded to visit the recycling bins! Schools and the media keep us informed of the many issues involved, but this does make it harder to cover the same ground in a distinctively Christian way. This outline takes a different approach, from the point of view of God's involvement in Creation.

1) 'Big Bang' theories are widely propagated and largely accepted as an account of the start of the universe, though even the brilliant mind of Stephen Hawking accepts the possibility that some force or being may have caused such an event to occur. Whatever one's personal feelings about this, the Christian belief is clearly that, whatever the mechanism, creation was entirely God's initiative. A useful simple illustration of this is a pile of Lego bricks (or equivalent) which only take shape as a model if someone applies mind and hands to ordering them – a volunteer to do this will emphasise the point.

2) The trouble with Lego models is that they're basically static – they can only change if the modeller so decides. God has given the world the capacity to grow and develop, but this still depends on him, since he's the source of all life. A family pet is a better example of this (preferably one in a cage, owned by a child in the congregation). Animals may seem to have a mind of their own, but they need the care of their human owners to survive – if you ask, most children will be well aware of what's necessary to keep a pet healthy and happy. God has given us free will, but we still rely on him as the Author and Sustainer of Life.

3) In giving us free will, God knew the potential downside but was willing to take the risk that we would go our own way. Still using the pet as an example, ask what would

happen if it escaped or got lost. Whatever answers you receive, no one will argue with you that it might be at great risk if it's not found quickly. You may know a personal story along these lines, or you can use Jesus' parable of the lost sheep, but bring out very clearly the idea of God saving and healing those he created. Point out, too, that in Greek the word for 'saviour' and 'healer' is the same.

4) Conclude by explaining that when God saves and heals he also restores. When the lost pet is found, it may need veterinary attention, but thereafter it will resume its place in the home. God also brings us back to where we should have been, and enables us to start off again as he intended us to and as Jesus showed us how.

SUNDAY NEXT BEFORE LENT

The Transfiguration is kept as a separate festival on 6th August, but it clearly has a place in the approach to Easter with its foreshadowing of Jesus' Passion and death. The ASB put it on the Fourth Sunday of Lent, but in most churches this conflicts with Mothering Sunday. The Revised Common Lectionary includes it on the Second Sunday of Lent with an alternative suggestion of today, the Sunday before Ash Wednesday, but the new lectionary establishes it here, providing a springboard into the themes of Lent and Passiontide. The Gospel readings for each of the three years describe the transfiguration of Jesus, not necessarily the simplest concept to convey to an all-age congregation, but one which opens our eyes to his majesty and glory as well as his humanity.

Hymns

TRADITIONAL

- *Christ, whose glory fills the skies*
- *God of grace and God of glory*
- *The Lord is King!*
- *Thy kingdom come, O God*
- *We hail thy presence glorious*

MODERN

- *Be still, for the presence of the Lord*
- *He is exalted*
- *Jesus shall take the highest honour*
- *Lord, the light of your love*
- *When I look into your holiness*

Readings

Year A   Exodus 24:12-18; 2 Peter 1:16-21; Matthew 17:1-9

Year B   2 Kings 2:1-12; 2 Corinthians 4:3-6; Mark 9:2-9

Year C   Exodus 34:29-35; 2 Corinthians 3:12-4:2; Luke 9:28-36 (37-43)

Confession

Coming into the presence of God's glory
as we see it in Jesus Christ,
we acknowledge our own unworthiness,
saying,
Merciful Lord, forgive our sins,
and make us worthy of you.

We have heard your words of life,
yet often our own lips have failed
to declare your glory.
Merciful Lord, forgive our sins,
and make us worthy of you.

We have seen your mighty works,
yet often our own hands have failed
to do your will.
Merciful Lord, forgive our sins,
and make us worthy of you.

We have seen your acts of compassion,
yet often our own hearts have failed
to respond
to the needs of those around us.
Merciful Lord, forgive our sins,
and make us worthy of you.

We have known your glorious presence,
yet often our own lives have failed
to be transformed.
Merciful Lord, forgive our sins,
and make us worthy of you.
Accept our penitence,
cleanse us of our sin,
and strengthen us in the service
of Jesus Christ, our Lord. Amen.

Absolution

God our Father,
whose glory is revealed in his Son,
have mercy on you,
grant you pardon for all your sins,
and restore you to the joy of serving him
in the sure hope of eternal life,
through Christ our Lord. Amen.

Prayer

As Jesus' first disciples
saw him transfigured in majesty,
we pray that his glory may be seen in our lives

and in our world.
Lord of glory,
transform our lives.

Lord Jesus,
we pray that you will reveal your glory
in the Church,
seeking to serve you,
yet weakened by disunity
and the pressures of the world around.
May your light dispel the shadows
of confusion and division,
so that, united in love, your people
may bring your good news
to every community and culture.
Lord of glory,
transform our lives.

Lord Jesus,
we pray that you will reveal your glory
in the world,
struggling with problems
and full of sadness and misery.
May your light banish the darkness
of violence, poverty, discrimination
and selfishness,
so that all people may share equally
in the good things you have given us,
and live in peace and harmony.
Lord of glory,
transform our lives.

Lord Jesus,
we pray that you will reveal your glory
to those who contend with the hurt
of exploitation and abuse,
who can see no way to escape
from the prison of their pain.
May your light pierce the gloom of their despair,
so that they may trust in your unfailing love
to reassure them and guide them onwards.
Lord of glory,
transform their lives.

Lord Jesus,
we pray that you will reveal your glory
to those enduring ill-health of body or mind,
the frailty or indignity of old age,
or the silent grip of loneliness and isolation,
especially . . .
May your light shine on them,
bringing the comforting warmth

of your presence
and the healing of your touch.
Lord of glory,
transform their lives.

Lord Jesus,
we pray that you will reveal your glory
in us and through us to those we encounter
day by day in our family, community,
school and workplace.
May our lives display and reflect
your transforming power
wherever you place us.
Lord of glory,
**transform our lives
for the sake of your kingdom. Amen.**

All-age address

The Transfiguration is arguably one of the most difficult accounts in the Gospels to get to grips with, let alone convey to an all-age congregation. Even the three disciples present showed some confusion in their reactions, Peter to the fore as ever! This outline address puts the emphasis on recognising Jesus as both human and divine, and how both could be present in the same person. By way of preparation you'll need to find a few magazine pictures of well-known people (sports or TV stars, perhaps) in unfamiliar situations or guises, and, if you or others are willing, some 'before and after' photos, showing the difference made by longer or shorter hair, a beard, or contrasting clothes styles. You could also take a magazine photo and 'doctor' it slightly with a moustache or beard in felt-tip pen. (It's helpful to have pictures pasted on to a piece of stiff card so that they can be manipulated more easily.)

If you've 'disguised' a well-known personality's image like this, start off by asking if anyone recognises who's underneath. It's likely someone will guess correctly fairly quickly, but others may be more confused, depending on the success of your artwork! When they've been identified, point out that the person underneath is still the same, however much you've defaced their picture – the change is entirely on paper. People have tried to reinterpret Jesus in all kinds of ways, to make him fit their own image of him, but however hard they may try, they can't get rid of the real person underneath.

Next bring out a picture of a famous personality but not as they're normally seen – perhaps one taken in an unexpected context, or doing something far removed from their popular image – and ask for guesses as to who the celebrity is. Again, demonstrate that the person is just the same; it's simply that we have to revise our view of what they're like, having seen a different side of them. Jesus never tried to live up to people's expectations of him, but simply did his heavenly Father's will. If we force him to fit our own expectations we'll be disappointed, but by accepting him on his own terms we can see him for who he really is.

Finally, bring out the family photos, showing how much the subjects have changed over a number of years. It's still the same person, but we're viewing them at different stages in their lives, wearing different clothes or hairstyles, or standing in different places. We're seeing them 'in a different light'. That's how the disciples saw Jesus on the mountain. They knew he was still their teacher and friend, but now they recognised who he really was, God's own Son, the one he'd promised to send to put everything right. Occasionally, we catch a glimpse of the majesty and glory of God as we see him in Jesus, but we can't organise or force it. Only as we follow him and open our eyes, ears and hearts to him will we be able to experience him as he really is.

THE SUNDAYS AFTER TRINITY

We now enter a long spell of Ordinary Time, which officially starts on the day after Pentecost, although the following Sunday, the first after Pentecost, is always celebrated as Trinity Sunday. In practice the second Sunday after Pentecost is also the first to be kept as part of Ordinary Time, though the new lectionary reverts to the Book of Common Prayer's description of it as the First Sunday after Trinity. The ASB provided twenty-two Sundays after Pentecost (including Trinity Sunday) before the Last Sunday after Pentecost, which was always kept on the tenth Sunday before Christmas, thus providing for nine Sundays prior to Christmas. If Easter and therefore Pentecost fell relatively late, it was the latter Sundays after Pentecost which were omitted.

The new calendar has approached the Sundays before Advent rather differently, and thus brings the Sundays after Trinity to a close on the last Sunday in October (or 24th October when All Saints' Day falls on a Sunday). This means that the earlier Sundays (Propers 4 to 7) are now omitted in those years when Easter arrives in mid or late April. In addition, you'll need to remember that while the readings always relate to the date, the collect and post-communion prayer will be those for whichever Sunday after Trinity it is. For the Principal Service, the New Testament and Gospel readings continue to follow their sequences, but with the Old Testament there is the option either of semi-continuous readings, or of passages reflecting the Gospel – both are included here.

PROPER 4

Sunday between 29th May and 4th June inclusive
(if after Trinity Sunday)

This Sunday's readings will only be used when Easter falls towards the end of March. Year A's passage from Matthew concludes the Sermon on the Mount; Year B's from Mark contains an account of Jesus' disputes with the authorities over the Sabbath; while Year C's from Luke tells of the Roman centurion's faith. As these are very varied, an outline address is provided for Years A and C, while for Year B, the outline given for Proper 3 would be equally applicable.

Hymns

TRADITIONAL

- *Father of heaven, whose love profound*
- *Glorious things of thee are spoken*
- *Jesu, lover of my soul*
- *O God, our help in ages past*
- *We have a gospel to proclaim*

MODERN

- *Be still and know that I am God*
- *Be still, for the presence of the Lord*
- *God's Spirit is in my heart*
- *Lord, the light of your love*
- *You are beautiful*

Readings

Year A   Genesis 6:9-22, 7:24, 8:14-19 or
          Deuteronomy 11:18-21, 26-28;
          Romans 1:16-17, 3:22b-28 (29-31);
          Matthew 7:21-29
Year B   1 Samuel 3:1-10 (11-20) or
          Deuteronomy 5:12-15;
          2 Corinthians 4:5-12; Mark 2:23-3:6
Year C   1 Kings 18:20-21, (22-29), 30-39 or
          1 Kings 8:22-23, 41-43; Galatians 1:1-12;
          Luke 7:1-10

Confession

Holy God,
we come to you in repentance and sorrow,
recognising our sins and failings,
conscious that we need of your forgiveness.
Our thoughts have been far from you,
our words have not been governed by you,
and our actions have not been
under your control.
We are sorry, and humbly seek your forgiveness.
In your mercy take away our sin,
make us clean and pure,
and redirect our lives
by the power of your Spirit,
through your Son, our Saviour Jesus Christ.
Amen.

Absolution

God, whose mercy and grace are without limit,
hear the cry of your heart,
pardon and deliver you from all your sin,
and guide you through this life
to the eternal joys of the life to come,
through his Son Jesus Christ our Lord.
Amen.

Prayer

We come to God as our Sovereign,
praying for his will to be done and saying,
Lord, hear us and answer:
we ask this in your name.

We think of the world around us
with its wars and conflicts,
its greed and corruption,
its pain and misery, especially . . .
We pray for all victims of natural disaster,
inhuman cruelty and man-made tragedy,
and for those who dedicate their lives
to relieving suffering,
wherever it is encountered.
Give them strength to endure
and perseverance to overcome obstacles.
Lord, hear us and answer:
we ask this in your name.

We think of the leaders of the world,
including our own government,
as they grapple with the many confusing
and disturbing issues
raised by human rights, scientific research
and information technology.
We pray for those in authority
as they make decisions and enact laws.
Give them wisdom to know what is right,
and courage to practise it.
Lord, hear us and answer:
we ask this in your name.

We think of our local community,
and the different elements which make it up –
schools and nurseries,
medical centres and hospitals,
day centres and residential homes,
shops and offices.
We pray for those who live or work around us,
that your presence may comfort the suffering,
protect the weak and encourage
the downhearted.
Give us strength to live for you day by day.
Lord, hear us and answer:
we ask this in your name.

We think of the Church,
both national and local,
and for its worship and witness.
We pray for Church leaders,
those who sit on synods and committees,
those engaged in a public ministry
of teaching and preaching,
and those currently training for it
or testing their vocation.
Give all Christian people a commitment
to proclaiming your Gospel
and to serving you as one.
Lord, hear us and answer:
we ask this in your name.

We think of those we know who are suffering
as a result of ill-health, grief,
depression or anxiety.
We pray especially for . . .
Give them reassurance
that they are in your loving hands,
and confidence that you will be with them
in every situation.
Lord, hear us and answer:
we ask this in your name.

We think of our own lives this week
and the things we will do,
the people we will meet,
the places in which we will find ourselves.
Exciting or mundane, joyful or sad,
may your unfailing love be seen and felt
in every moment.
Lord hear us and answer:
we ask this in your name,
and for the sake of your Son,
Jesus Christ our Lord. Amen.

All-age address 1

This first outline is based on Jesus' parable of
the wise and foolish builders, and makes the
point that the principles of constructing a
building also apply to the Christian life. It
needs a fair amount of preparation, plus a
willingness to think bigger than usual and
take a few risks! You'll need a reasonably large
sandpit, several large jugs of water, a bucket
and spade, and some bricks (real, as opposed
to the children's toy version). A number of
volunteers are needed to help with the
demonstration; age is irrelevant but younger
ones will probably be more enthusiastic.

1) First, ask two assistants to make a sand castle
using the bucket and spade. As they do this,
compliment the quality of their work. When
it's finished, ask two more to pour a jug or
two of water over it, as violently as possible.
It won't take long for it to start washing
away. Either consult the congregation about
the problem or point out yourself that good
foundations and durable materials are a
prerequisite of a building that will last. Our
faith won't survive either, unless we base it
on Jesus Christ and on the spiritual things
that last for ever, rather than the material
goods of this world.

2) Now ask the volunteers to construct a wall
in the sandpit with the bricks (maybe a dozen
or so), and again pour water over them.
You'll certainly wash away any grains of
sand, but the bricks won't move. They aren't
especially beautiful in themselves but when
they're put together with other bricks to
make a house, the finished product can

look very smart and impressive – and it'll last! Jesus wants his hearers to understand that our faith must endure all the storms and stresses of this life, made of 'material' that will last (that is, putting his words into practice), and put together in a coherent pattern. Spiritual maturity is seen in a faith and a Church that can weather the difficulties and opposition and stand firm.

All-age address 2

This outline looks at the question of faith from the perspective of Luke's account of the healing of the centurion's servant. Considerable distress has sometimes been caused by the suggestion that such healing is invariably and directly linked to the amount of faith on display, and, while Jesus commends the centurion for his faith, this is more to show up the lack of faith among the Jews than to indicate the circumstances under which he's willing to heal. There are several effective ways to illustrate faith.

1) Invite a volunteer to come and sit on a chair. The mere fact of the invitation may arouse suspicions as to whether it's safe or not, but an element of trust is necessary when sitting on any chair! Admittedly, this isn't entirely a matter of faith as visual evidence and past experience help us decide if a particular chair is reliable, but make the point that however much we talk about it, faith is seen in the act of sitting down. The centurion knew of Jesus' reputation, and may even have discussed it with his friends, but Jesus knew his faith was real by his action in sending a message to him.

2) Another test of faith is to ask a volunteer to fall over and trust that they will be caught – the most effective method is to ask four other volunteers in advance to link hands in a circle and catch the person in the middle as they fall and return them to an upright position, so that the process can be repeated. Children are far more trusting than adults at this exercise! Stress that the element of faith is far more real now, but that the more the one in the middle is caught by the others, the more trust they'll build up. The more

we put our trust in God, the more we'll discover he's completely faithful and never lets us down. That's how our faith is strengthened.

3) Offer a pound coin (or however much you think appropriate, though don't go too low or no one will think it's worth the effort!) to anyone in the congregation who's willing to come and take it from you. Amazingly, most people will think there's a catch in it somewhere, except younger children, whose parents may well try instead to restrain them at this point. The worst-case scenario is half the congregation queuing up for it, so make sure you know your limit! Faith in this case means taking someone at their word, believing they'll keep their promise and receiving what they're offering. The centurion believed Jesus meant what he said, that he would keep his word, and so he acted on it. As a result the thing he most wanted happened – his favourite servant was healed.

PROPER 5

Sunday between 5th and 11th June inclusive
(if after Trinity Sunday)

From now until the end of October the readings run in sequence, and while it wouldn't be possible to read each Gospel in its entirety (this wouldn't be necessary anyway if accounts common to two or all three of them are taken into consideration), the coverage is fairly comprehensive. Year A's passage from Matthew is in two parts – the story of the calling of Matthew, and the healing of a woman with a haemorrhage and of a young girl who had just died. In Year B the passage from Mark consists of the dispute over Jesus' authority to cast out demons, while Year C's from Luke recounts the raising of the widow's son.

Hymns

TRADITIONAL

- *A brighter dawn is breaking*
- *Come, ye faithful, raise the anthem*
- *Father of heaven, whose love profound*
- *Immortal love, for ever full*
- *There's a wideness in God's mercy*

MODERN

- *Be still and know that I am God*
- *Christ's is the world*
- *Only by grace can we enter*
- *When God Almighty came to earth*
- *Will you come and follow me*

Readings

Year A   Genesis 12:1-9 or Hosea 5:15-6:6;
          Romans 4:13-25; Matthew 9:9-13, 18-26
Year B   1 Samuel 8:4-11, (12-15), 16-20,
          (11:14-15) or Genesis 3:8-15;
          2 Corinthians 4:13-5:1; Mark 3:20-35
Year C   1 Kings 17:8-16 or 17-24;
          Galatians 1:11-24; Luke 7:11-17

Confession

Lord of all,
in your holy presence we kneel in penitence,
knowing that our lips are impure,
our hands unclean,
our hearts unfit to come near you.
We are sorry and ashamed
of all our wrongdoing,
and ask you to forgive our waywardness
and self-centredness.
Have mercy on us,
wash away all our sins,
and by your grace make us worthy
to stand before you and serve your kingdom,
through Jesus Christ our Saviour.
Amen.

Absolution

Almighty God,
whose power can heal the sick
and raise the dead
have mercy on you,
forgive all your sins,
heal your backsliding,
and raise you to a new and eternal life,
through his Son Jesus Christ, our risen Lord.
Amen.

Prayer

God calls us to hear his voice
and respond to his love
in joyful worship and loving service.
We bring him our concerns and requests
for the Church, the world and those in need,
saying,
Lord, receive this our prayer;
hear and answer us, we pray.

Lord, your Church is threatened
by many different factors –
persecution and apathy from the outside,
disunity and confusion within.
Encourage and bless all Christians
who face physical and mental torment
or even death for their faith;
motivate those who despair
at the lack of interest in you;

bind together all who name Christ as Lord
and strengthen them in your service.
Especially we pray . . .
Lord, receive this our prayer;
hear and answer us, we pray.

Lord, this world is in turmoil,
and insecurity rules our lives.
Hostility and violence are ever-present;
poverty and economic chaos
degrade many lives;
pollution and greed continue
to scar the face of your creation;
dishonesty and corruption
bring leadership into disrepute.
Give wisdom to governments and authorities
to lead us in the right paths,
and empower all those who struggle
for peace and justice.
Especially we pray . . .
Lord, receive this our prayer;
hear and answer us, we pray.

Lord, many suffering people
need the touch of your loving hand –
the elderly and infirm,
the jobless and homeless,
the abused and violated,
the physically and mentally ill,
the grieving and the despairing.
Bring them relief from their troubles
and healing from their pain,
and, through those who care about them,
show them the depth of your compassion.
Especially we pray . . .
Lord, receive this our prayer;
hear us and answer, we pray.

Lord, we too need you day by day,
in work and leisure,
in community and solitude,
in waking and sleeping.
Stay with us as friend,
go with us as guide
and be present with us always
that we may live in your strength
and rest in your love.
Lord, receive this our prayer;
hear us and answer, we pray,
for the sake of your kingdom. Amen.

All-age address 1

The issue of life after death was somewhat controversial in Jesus' time, and viewed by Jewish traditionalists as a trendy, even dangerous new idea, which enabled Paul to make effective use of a split among his opponents (Acts 23:7-8). The accounts of Jesus' resuscitation of the dead in two of these Gospel readings must have caused consternation among the religious authorities. It might be argued that the little girl had only just died (not much consolation when there's no casualty unit or emergency treatment available) but the widow's son had evidently been dead long enough for the funeral to be in progress. Contemporary society tries to shy away from death, or failing that to talk about it ad nauseam. It would be tempting to argue that as a subject it isn't suitable for all-age worship, but in the context of resurrection and new life it's fundamental to the Christian faith. Here are three ways to illustrate the Christian understanding of death.

1) Take a pot-plant which looks dead in winter (a fuchsia is an excellent example) and point out that only a few weeks previously it looked brown and dead, with no sign of life. It's certainly true that last year's flowers, leaves and branches have died, so that this year's growth truly is new life, which wouldn't be possible unless the old had died. As Christians we recognise that our bodies, the visible sign that we're alive, inevitably deteriorate and die. However, in Christ, who defeated death by his resurrection, we are restored to the eternal life for which our heavenly Father created us and which sin destroyed. Our old earthly life has to finish so that we can enter into the far better one which lies ahead.

2) Obtain a couple of house sale leaflets from an estate agent, and as you display them or read a few details out, ask who's moved house recently. Explain that major changes like this in our lives can often feel like a bereavement (leaving a school or job are similar experiences). However, if we don't 'die' to our old life in that house or school, we can't start another one in a new house, a new job or at university. Christians believe that even while

we remain on this earth we have a foretaste of what that new life after death will be like, when we can enjoy God's presence for ever and be what he made us to be.

3) Finally bring out a baby's training beaker, a child's plastic drinking glass, a chunky mug and a bone china cup. Show that there's a development here, from a small child learning to drink without spilling any, to a child learning to drink from a normal mug that won't break if it's dropped, to the sort of mug that adorns most university and college rooms. Finally, bring out the best bone china crockery. As each stage of growing up to adulthood is reached, so the signs of the previous phase are left behind – we don't expect grown-ups to use plastic training beakers, though no doubt they once did! In moving on to each new stage of life, we 'die' to the old with its immaturity and limited scope. As Christians, we die to our old life with its sins, weaknesses and limitations, so that we can move on to something better. Jesus' miracles were a picture of how, through his death and resurrection, we can receive new life, which enables us to die to the old. In him, as those around him realised very well, a whole new perspective on life and death was being opened up.

All-age address 2

The passage from Mark, describing how the Pharisees accused Jesus of casting out demons through Beelzebub, is one of the hardest in all the Gospels to understand. We no longer think in those terms, but underlying their criticism is one question which everyone will understand – what gives Jesus the authority to do and say what he does? The last thing the religious leaders wanted was for him to be recognised as acting solely on God's authority. So they accused him instead of invoking the powers of darkness to exorcise demons and evil spirits, a quite ludicrous argument, as Jesus quickly demonstrated. For this address you'll need just a few symbols of authority, such as a police officer's cap or helmet, a passport, an ID tag permitting access to a building, a pantomime crown or tiara, and a doctor's white coat and stethoscope.

1) Police officers are employed to ensure the rest of us obey the laws of the country, and to help people who are in difficulty or danger. If we see a blue light flashing we know we must stop or drive more slowly; if the police have sealed an area off we aren't allowed to go there. Most people don't argue with police officers for very long! But their authority comes from the law itself, and they themselves are subject to it.

2) A passport is important to enable us to travel in other countries. Show the message from Her Majesty in the front cover to the rulers of other nations. When we go to those places we do so with that authority in our passport, not just because we thought it would be a nice thing to do.

3) An ID tag provides authorisation to be in a particular place, usually from the owner, because we have the right to be there, or have to be as part of our work.

4) A doctor's coat and stethoscope shows that this person is skilled, trained and authorised to handle certain drugs, prescribe courses of treatment, or even to carry out surgery. Before they can function as doctors they must pass exams and be accepted by the medical authorities as able to do their work to the necessary standards.

5) A crown is the ultimate symbol of authority, as all the other examples derive their authority from someone or something else. But where does a king get his authority from? No earthly ruler can govern without his authority coming from God – that's quite different from self-appointed power. Jesus is King of kings, yet he was quite clear that everything he did was in obedience to his heavenly Father. The religious leadership of his day refused to recognise that, but their refusal led them to making absurd and blasphemous suggestions which meant they were turning their backs totally on God in order to protect their own reputation. In so doing they were showing everyone that Jesus' authority was greater because it came straight from his Father.

PROPER 6

Sunday between 12th and 18th June inclusive
(if after Trinity Sunday)

As the Gospel readings settle into their sequential pattern it may seem that significant chunks are being omitted. Even allowing for the infancy and Passion narratives, Matthew and Luke are too long to be fitted into twenty-five weeks of readings, while some material is common to two or all three synoptic Gospels. In the Gospel for Year A Matthew tells of Jesus' need for more co-workers, and the sending out of the disciples; Year B sees Mark describing two parables of the kingdom; while in Year C Luke recounts Jesus' anointing by a sinful woman, and adds a few verses about the women who followed Jesus.

Hymns

TRADITIONAL

- *All my hope on God is founded*
- *All people that on earth do dwell*
- *Love divine, all loves excelling*
- *My faith looks up to thee*
- *The Church's one foundation*

MODERN

- *Alleluia, alleluia, give thanks to the risen Lord*
- *Come on and celebrate*
- *I am a new creation*
- *I'm accepted, I'm forgiven*
- *Jubilate, everybody*

Readings

Year A   Genesis 18:1-15 (21:1-7) or
Exodus 19:2-8a; Romans 5:1-8;
Matthew 9:35-10:8 (9-23)

Year B   1 Samuel 15:34-16:13 or
Ezekiel 17:22-24; 2 Corinthians 5:6-10
(11-13) 14-17; Mark 4:26-34

Year C   1 Kings 21:1-10 (11-14) 15-21a or
2 Samuel 11:26-12:10, 13-15;
Galatians 2:15-21; Luke 7:36-8:3

Confession

Lord God, our Creator,
we come to you acknowledging our sinfulness
and seeking your forgiveness, saying,
Lord, have mercy on us;
cleanse us and make us whole.

We repent of unwise or unkind words
we have spoken,
causing hurt and anger.
Lord, have mercy on us;
cleanse us and make us whole.

We repent of selfish or thoughtless actions
we have committed,
causing needless misery and irritation.
Lord, have mercy on us;
cleanse us and make us whole.

We repent of unfair or judgemental
attitudes we hold,
causing us to speak unfairly and act unjustly.
Lord, have mercy on us;
cleanse us and make us whole.

We repent of all that falls short
of your standards,
asking you to forgive all our sins
and give us strength to live for your glory.
Lord, have mercy on us;
**cleanse us and make us whole,
through Jesus Christ our Lord. Amen.**

Absolution

God our Father,
who loves all he has created,
grant you pardon and deliverance
from all your sins,
peace in your hearts,
and the joy of new life
through Christ our Lord. Amen.

Prayer

As members of God's kingdom,
we come to Jesus
with our requests and prayers, saying,
Lord, may your kingdom grow;
reign in our hearts, we pray.

Bless and guide your people
throughout the world
who are faced with the threats
of persecution and ill-treatment,
or marginalisation and apathy.
Give strength to the suffering,
encouragement to the downhearted,
and unite us all in your service
through your love.
Lord, may your kingdom grow;
reign in your Church we pray.

Bless and guide the Church
in our local community
as we seek to address the issues around,
especially . . .
Give us courage to overcome
the barriers of the past,
to join together in your name,
and leave behind unimportant issues,
so that together we can work
to bring your good news to the world.
Lord, may your kingdom grow;
reign in our church, we pray.

Bless and guide the governments of the world
as they face the challenges
of deprivation and poverty,
disputes and violence.
Give them discernment to make good decisions,
boldness to confront corruption and vice,
and wisdom to act for the good of all people.
Lord, may your kingdom grow;
reign in our world, we pray.

Bless and guide our families,
friends and loved ones,
in particular those going through dark times
or facing tough decisions, especially . . .
Give them comfort and peace
in their suffering,
healing of body and mind,
and confidence that you will be alongside,
bringing them the hope of eternal life.
Lord, may your kingdom grow;
reign in their lives, we pray.

Bless and guide us at school
or in the workplace,
among family and friends,
and in our neighbourhood,
and give us commitment to live for you

and proclaim your love wherever we are.
Lord, may your kingdom grow;
**reign in our hearts
and help us live for your glory,
for the sake of your Son,
our Saviour Jesus Christ. Amen.**

All-age address 1

This outline is based on the sending out of the disciples, making use of the fact that most people are familiar with receiving orders to fulfil particular tasks or objectives. You'll need to prepare five envelopes with instructions inside, which need to cover the following points: 1) there's work to be done and too few people to do it; 2) the order carries authority for it to be fulfilled; 3) it must be carried out single-mindedly; 4) it won't be easy and there'll be opposition; 5) there needs to be a report back. Given the importance of social concern in Christian mission, a task based on this is suggested, though if you collect money make sure people know exactly which good cause it will go to. In the interests of time it's preferable for this to be completed after the service, with a report back at the next suitable opportunity. The outline is based around this idea, although another idea may be more appropriate for different circumstances.

1) Prime two 'volunteers' before the service (if possible children or teenagers), and, having called them out, emphasise the importance of their 'unique skills of persuasion and charm'! Ask them to open the first envelope, which will underline this point, saying that there's plenty of money in people's wallets and purses, but no one else to make a collection for the charity in question. As a pair they must help and support each other in their work. Jesus also sent the disciples out to do his work because there was no one else willing to do it, and Luke tells us he sent them in pairs, to learn how to work co-operatively.

2) The next envelope should contain a signed authorisation from the vicar or most senior minister present, entitling these two people to make a collection on behalf of the church

for the chosen charity. As Jesus' followers we don't engage in ministry for lack of anything better to do, nor because we think it's a good idea. All Christian ministry comes under God's authority, and only if we do it in his name will it be worthwhile.

3) The third envelope should say that the volunteers must concentrate on this and nothing else, taking nothing with them except their own commitment and their authorisation. Jesus knew the disciples would be distracted very easily, so he didn't allow them to take any spare clothes or cash, or even food – they were to fulfil their task single-mindedly and trust God to supply all their needs.

4) The fourth envelope should contain a 'health warning' – this task won't be easy. Not everyone will be so willing to make a donation, and some might even be rude when they're asked. Jesus didn't want his disciples to be under any illusions either about the arduous nature of the work, nor about the likely response in some places. We shouldn't be naive or unrealistic, but Christian ministry isn't based on fulfilling certain 'success criteria'. Rather we're called to faithful proclamation of the good news and loving service to those in need.

5) The final envelope holds the date for feedback on how the work has gone. Luke tells us that the disciples returned joyfully to tell all that had happened. British reserve notwithstanding, we shouldn't be afraid to declare where and how we've seen God at work in the world, and share our own joy at the way his kingdom is growing.

All-age address 2

The second outline is based on Jesus' kingdom parables in Mark 4 (though it serves those in Matthew 13 equally well). The particular illustration here is of growth in the natural world, but this focuses more generally on the nature of God's kingdom. It requires only a few basic props, and assumes that at least a few of the congregation will have had experience of a foreign business trip or holiday at some time.

Beforehand you'll need to find or borrow a passport, some leftover foreign coins, a red warning triangle, a phrase-book and, if possible, a history of a country you're familiar with.

Begin by asking if anyone's been abroad recently, and follow this up with a question about what makes being abroad different from living in the British Isles. You may find it helpful to write up the suggested differences on an OHP slide or flip-chart. The suggestions you get will certainly include:

1) *People may speak a different language.* Produce the phrase-book and read out a couple of amusing or striking phrases in the language concerned. While it may not matter for a short trip, if we're to engage with those people on a regular or serious level we must learn to speak their language. In God's kingdom there's a quite different 'language' to the one in this world. Words like 'materialism', 'racism', 'abuse' and 'selfishness' don't exist. If we're part of God's kingdom we'll learn words like 'caring', 'compassion', 'integrity' and 'love' instead. If you've found a suitable history book, use it to explain that even countries which speak our language have a different culture and way of looking at life. The basic attitudes of God's kingdom are quite alien to much of what we find in the rest of the world.

2) *There's a different currency.* Here you can display the coins. Explain that things may be more or less expensive in other countries. God's kingdom has values quite distinct from those we'll mostly find in this world – in fact, it usually turns them upside down, as Jesus often demonstrated.

3) *There are different laws.* The red warning triangle is a useful and simple example, as (at the time of writing) UK law doesn't require one to be carried, whereas this is obligatory in many continental countries. God's laws are quite clearly described in the Bible, and again they're quite different to our human rules and regulations, because they're based on following the liberating way of Christ, rather than restricting what we can do and threatening punishment (you may like to refer to the latter part of Galatians 5).

4) *There's a different authority.* This is where the passport comes into its own. When we travel in another country we must obey its laws, but we carry the authority of the Queen to be there. As members of his kingdom, God is our final authority – all human authority comes from him, and it wouldn't be possible to legislate for or against his law of love. Jesus sets us the example of complete obedience to his Father's will, and we must follow his lead, which usually means complying with civil laws unless they're contrary to his commandments.

All-age address 3

Few people would argue that Luke shows a remarkable empathy with women throughout his Gospel, which surely reflects Jesus' own attitude and approach. From our twentieth-century perspective it's easy to forget how radical this was in its day – the disciples' reaction to Jesus talking at the well with a Samaritan woman suggests this would have been considered at best improper. However, gender isn't the main concern of the primary account here. Instead, Luke contrasts the attitude of the previously sinful woman with that of Simon, the self-righteous Pharisee, to show his readers that a forgiven sinner responds to God's love on a far deeper level than one who barely understands his need of forgiveness. To highlight this contrast, use an OHP slide or flip-chart divided into two columns, one for each character. If you're able to draw or have access to a good cartoonist, you could do this with pictures rather than words.

1) The two words here are *affectionate* and *detached*. The woman showed how she felt about Jesus by weeping and kissing his feet, while Simon hadn't even offered him the greeting of a kiss. Sinful she may have been, but the woman responded to Jesus' love and wasn't bothered what anyone else thought, even if Simon and the other guests were more concerned about him being 'contaminated' by the touch of a sinner.

2) The next two words might be *generous* and *mean*. The woman was willing to use an expensive jar of perfume to wash Jesus' feet, whereas Simon hadn't extended him the courtesy of water to clean his feet when he'd arrived. The perfume may have been a symbol of her past life but now it's dedicated to and used on Jesus.

3) Now write up the words *accepting* and *disapproving*. The woman showed her total acceptance of Jesus by pouring the perfume over him, unlike Simon who showed no willingness even to pour olive oil (which was much less expensive) on his guest's head, a sign of recognition and welcome.

4) The final words could be *forgiven* and *self-righteous*. The woman recognised her need of forgiveness, but Simon and his friends seemed not to have the slightest idea that they might have done anything wrong which would require God to forgive them.

Simon did what was expected of a host, but no more. The woman gave the best she knew to Jesus in response to his love and forgiveness. The more we recognise how much we've been forgiven, the easier it is to express our love for him and commitment to following his ways. The Pharisees' problem was that they looked down their noses at the sinners with whom Jesus associated, and quite failed to see that in God's eyes they too needed to be forgiven. The woman, whatever her past, went home forgiven because she'd demonstrated her faith in Jesus by her action.

PROPER 7

Sunday between 19th and 25th June inclusive
(if after Trinity Sunday)

This is the last of the four Sundays after Trinity which may be omitted, if Easter falls fairly late in April. Matthew continues in Year A with last week's Gospel reading, as Jesus tells the disciples the cost of following him; Mark, in Year B, has the account of Jesus calming the storm; and in Year C Luke describes the healing of an uncontrollable demoniac. Two outline addresses are suggested for Years A and B. The Year C Gospel isn't easy for younger members of the congregation to comprehend, but the points from Year B about Jesus' lordship can readily be adapted.

Hymns

TRADITIONAL

- *As pants the hart for cooling streams*
- *Be still, my soul*
- *Great is thy faithfulness*
- *Jesu, lover of my soul*
- *Praise, my soul, the King of heaven*

MODERN

- *As the deer pants for the water*
- *Give thanks with a grateful heart*
- *Inspired by love and anger*
- *There are hundreds of sparrows*
- *When God Almighty came to earth*

Readings

Year A   Genesis 21:8-21 or Jeremiah 20:7-13; Romans 6:1b-11; Matthew 10:24-39

Year B   1 Samuel 17:(1a, 4-11, 19-23) 32-49 or 17:57-18:5, 10-16 or Job 38:1-11; 2 Corinthians 6:1-13; Mark 4:35-41

Year C   1 Kings 19:1-4 (5-7) 8-15a or Isaiah 65:1-9; Galatians 3:23-29; Luke 8:26-39

Confession

Lord Jesus,
full of compassion and mercy,
you receive gladly all who come to you
in penitence and faith.
We are truly sorry
that we have fallen short of your standards,
and have lived according to human wisdom
instead of putting our trust in you.
Forgive our sins, we ask you,
and help us put the past behind us
so that we may walk with you
in newness of life,
for your name's sake. Amen.

Absolution

God our Father,
the unchanging and all-merciful Lord,
have mercy on you,
forgive all your sins
and take away your guilt
for the sake of his Son,
our Saviour Jesus Christ. Amen.

Prayer

We stand in the presence of our risen Lord
with many burdens and concerns.
As we offer them to him we pray,
Jesus, stand among us
in your risen power.

Touch with your healing hand, Lord Jesus,
the broken places of our world:
city streets inhabited by homeless children,
shanty towns concealing gross poverty,
communities wearied and scarred
by violence and insecurity,
countries torn apart by war and famine.
Open our eyes to their pain
and fill us with compassion
to respond with loving service.
Jesus, stand among us
in your risen power.

Touch with your gentle Spirit, Lord Jesus,
our confused and divided Church:
Christians separated by age-old barriers,
time spent on fruitless discussion
rather than proclaiming your good news,

little effective witness to your transforming love.
Open our minds to the riches
of your kingdom,
help us to learn of you from one another,
and to work together for your glory.
Jesus, stand among us
in your risen power.

Touch with your loving presence, Lord Jesus,
those whose lives are darkened
by the shadow of suffering:
illness or infirmity,
depression or mental anguish,
breakdown of relationships,
the loneliness of bereavement,
or rejection by others.
We remember especially . . .
Open our hearts to comfort and help them,
and our hands to ease their burden.
Jesus, stand among us
in your risen power.

Touch with your risen power, Lord Jesus,
our daily lives:
our relationships with those we love,
our routine contacts with other people,
our times of being active and busy,
our times of relaxation and quiet.
Keep our hearts and lives open
to receive your blessing,
our hands and hearts to share your love
with those around us,
and fix our eyes on you,
the Author and Perfecter of our faith.
Jesus, stand among us
in your risen power,
and fill our hearts with hope and joy,
for your name's sake. Amen.

All-age address 1

Jesus' words about the cost of discipleship are
as tough and uncompromising as any he uttered
– the idea that Christianity is an escape-route
from the reality of normal life would have cut
no ice with him! The aim of this address is to
demonstrate how anything that's truly worthwhile will cost us not only in cash terms, but
also in time, energy, and maybe even changing
the way we think and act. Preparation is
straightforward, requiring only the simplest of
props.

1) If you don't own one yourself, obtain a
copy of the latest hit CD – it should be easy
enough to find a teenager who's bought it
already and is willing to loan it for the
service. Holding it up for all to see, ask if
anyone else has got theirs yet. No doubt
some will say they have, but others may
say they can't afford it, or are saving up
pocket-money. The point is unmissable –
nothing comes free. The artists and technical
staff have to be paid, the raw materials paid
for, distribution and storage costs covered –
and, after all that, everyone involved wants
to make a profit. So we have to work or
save up to pay for it.

2) Now display a holiday brochure, ideally for
somewhere exotic or expensive. Ask if anyone's visited this place, and point out that
most of us don't have sufficient funds just
to go and pay for the holiday. In fact for
most of us it would be the trip of a lifetime,
and we'd have to work very hard for a long
time to be able to afford it. But, if we did so,
we'd probably regard the effort, time and
cost involved as well worthwhile.

3) Finally, show a degree or diploma certificate,
and find out if anyone has something similar.
Point out that while we might have to pay for
tuition fees, money can't buy us a successful
result. That only comes from working and
giving up our time and energy to this one
objective, perhaps even overcoming the
objections of others, but when we see the
certificate we realise that it was all worth it.

Conclude by explaining how Jesus was making
similar points to those who wanted to follow
him. The Christian life isn't a hobby for people
who like that kind of thing, or who need
something to occupy their time. It will cost
those who follow the way of Jesus in time,
effort and commitment – and probably money
too! The most important and valuable things
in life don't come cheaply or easily. It cost
Jesus everything, even his life, to win for us
forgiveness and new life, and as his disciples
we must expect our way to be tough at times.
It's in coming through the difficulties and
hardships that we recognise that the effort and
pain was worth enduring.

All-age address 2

Many people have sought power over the course of human history, but the extreme measures they've taken to try and hold on to it strongly suggest a deep-seated fear of losing control. No one has exerted a more powerful influence on history than Jesus Christ, but he never made any attempt even to gain a position of power, let alone hang on to it. His contemporaries were astonished at his control, but he seemed not to need to manipulate people or situations to his own advantage. The story of the calming of the sea is a good example. This outline looks briefly at human pictures of power, contrasting them with the way Jesus exercised it.

1) Begin by displaying a weather map or forecast, ideally with a good variety of different conditions on it – hot and sunny, rainy and windy, cold and frosty. Say that meteorologists are becoming increasingly good at predicting the weather, but they can't actually control it. No doubt farmers, sporting figures and holidaymakers would be delighted if they could! Possessing information doesn't automatically imply control over a situation. Maybe Jesus knew a storm was brewing; maybe he recommended that everyone take wet weather gear. But what stunned the disciples was his lordship over the elements, a demonstration that the Creator God had become part of his own creation.

2) Now exhibit a photograph, or better still a collage of photos, of various well-known political figures, asking for their identities. All politicians want us to believe they can get the country under control, sort out international crises and make us all millionaires! Once they're elected, however, the story is usually rather different. Some become interested only in their own image, some find they simply can't cope under the pressure, while others distort the truth in order to remain popular. Jesus, here as elsewhere, is in full command of the situation, even though he appears to be totally unaware of it! He shows no signs of stress, no concern for image or popularity, and retains his integrity.

3) The final illustration should be a photo of a great human achievement which involved conquering fear – a round-the-world sailing voyage would be an ideal example. Those who take part in such adventures have to learn to overcome their fears if they're to succeed in their aim. Few things are more intractable or harder to bring under control than deep-seated fears, but Jesus here wipes out the disciples' terror, chiding them for their lack of faith in him. Within a few seconds their only fear is of his awesome power.

Conclude by emphasising that all creation is under God's control, that no situation is beyond his scope, and that his perfect love will remove even our deepest fears. The same points can be made, with slightly different applications, to Luke's account of the healing of the demoniac.

PROPER 8

Sunday between 26th June and 2nd July inclusive

The summer holiday season isn't far away now. In schools most of the exams will be over and the term coming to an end; at work many people will be organising themselves to take a week or two's break; however, seaside resorts and tourist locations will be gearing themselves up for the peak season. Many worshippers will be looking forward to a few weeks of less frenetic activity, and even if your church is in a holiday area don't forget that you may have many extra visitors who will be looking for relaxation and refreshment. But the challenge of the Gospel isn't reduced! The reading from Matthew 10 for Year A finishes a long section on discipleship, while in Year B we read Mark's familiar story combining an unexpected healing with the raising from death of a young girl. Year C's reading from Luke returns to the cost of following Jesus, for which a suitable address outline can be found for Proper 7.

Hymns

TRADITIONAL

- *Amazing grace*
- *Be thou my vision*
- *Dear Lord and Father of mankind*
- *New every morning is the love*
- *O Lord, my God*

MODERN

- *Abba, Father, let me be*
- *All that I am*
- *Cry 'Freedom!'*
- *Moses, I know you're the man*
- *Will you come and follow me*

Readings

Year A   Genesis 22:1-14 or Jeremiah 28:5-9;
           Romans 6:12-23; Matthew 10:40-42
Year B   2 Samuel 1:1, 17-27 or
           Wisdom of Solomon 1:13-15, 2:23-24
           or Lamentations 3:23-33;
           2 Corinthians 8:7-15; Mark 5:21-43
Year C   2 Kings 2:1-2, 6-14 or
           1 Kings 19:15-16, 19-21;
           Galatians 5:1, 13-25; Luke 9:51-62

Confession

Loving Father,
you call us to be free,
but we have misused the freedom you give.
We have indulged our selfish desires
instead of serving one another;
we have criticised and condemned
instead of encouraging;
we have become arrogant and proud
instead of serving humbly.
We are sorry and ashamed,
and repent of all we have done wrong.
Forgive us, we pray,
and renew us by your Spirit,
that our lives may bear fruit for your glory,
through our Saviour, Jesus Christ. Amen.

Absolution

God our Maker,
whose very nature is love,
have mercy on you,
forgive all your sins,
and give you grace to walk with him
in step with his Spirit,
through Jesus Christ our Lord. Amen.

Prayer

We call to the Lord
who has lifted us from the depths,
offering him our prayers for the Church
and the world and saying,
Hear us, O Lord, and be merciful;
O Lord, be our help.

We call to you, our Father,
praying for your worldwide Church,
in some places facing opposition
and persecution,
in others struggling against apathy
and cynicism,
elsewhere coping with severely
limited resources.

In particular we bring to you . . .
Bless and guide Christian leaders
of all traditions,
in national roles or local congregations,
and inspire all Christian people,
to spread your good news
throughout the world.
Hear us, O Lord, and be merciful;
O Lord, be our help.

We call to you, Lord Jesus,
praying for our whole earth,
with its environmental exploitation,
international tensions, rank injustice
and desperate poverty.
In particular we bring to you . . .
Give wisdom to all governmental
leaders and agencies,
business directors and media controllers,
that they may pursue the paths
of truth and peace,
and courage to all Christian people
to uphold your standards.
Hear us, O Lord, and be merciful;
O Lord, be our help.

We call to you, Holy Spirit,
praying for anyone we know
who is enduring illness of body or mind,
caring for infirm or elderly loved ones,
or facing difficult decisions.
In particular we commend
to your loving care . . .
Give them strength
to see through their time of testing,
and confidence to believe
that all things work together for good
to those who love God.
Hear us, O Lord, and be merciful;
O Lord, be our help.

We call to you, blessed Trinity,
praying that our faith
may be rooted in your word,
and visible in our lives day by day.
As we know your saving grace in our hearts,
may our lips and our lives declare your praises.
Hear us, O Lord, and be merciful;
**O Lord, be our help now
and our joy for evermore. Amen.**

All-age address 1

Although the last three verses of Matthew 10 are so brief, they're profound enough to warrant an address outline in their own right. This one focuses on possible responses to Jesus and the disciples he's sent out in his name. The only props needed are magazine advertisements, articles, headlines or pictures.

1) Find an advert or two with a clear message (and large enough to be visible), and either paste them on to separate pieces of card or form them into a collage. Ask for suggestions about what the message might be – advertisers are rarely very subtle! Point out that just as they want us to understand what they're saying, so God wants us to be clear about his message too. That's why he sent the prophets, though many refused to listen to them. Nor were Jesus' contemporaries always willing to hear him explain what God was saying. That's why Jesus says here that listening to God's message through his servants is just as important as giving it.

2) Now select a few headlines or brief words extolling someone who's behaved courageously or commendably. Having sought views about what was praiseworthy in these, point out that the media frequently emphasise bad news, even making cynical comments about 'do-gooders'. This is in marked contrast to Jesus' words, which indicate how highly God values those who accept and encourage righteousness and justice.

3) Jesus' own illustration of a cup of cold water is simple and clear, though it needs expanding for our culture. It may seem rather paltry to us, but what matters is the public gesture of support for those who speak God's words and do his works. In receiving and accepting them, we're opening ourselves to our heavenly Father and accepting him too. You might conclude by seeking support (with money and prayer) for a Christian worker in difficult circumstances.

All-age address 2

Mark's account of the raising of Jairus' daughter is also one of his longest, mainly because on his way to the house Jesus was delayed both by the crowds who wanted to see him and by a very persistent woman. Having described the healing of the demoniac, a man beyond his own or anyone else's ability to control, Mark now introduces us to a young girl on her death-bed, and a middle-aged woman the doctors had given up on. According to the understanding of those times, at least, no-one could do any more for them. He also contrasts the faith of the girl's father and the woman with the disinterest and scorn of those around. This outline looks at the way Jesus goes about ministering to them, using the mnemonic 'WHOLE'.

1) Although he's engaged in teaching the people when Jairus comes to him, Jesus responds immediately to the request, no doubt comforting the distraught father as they head towards his home. As a synagogue leader Jairus may have risked opposition from other religious folk for approaching Jesus like this, but although it's the only hope left he clearly believes Jesus can heal his daughter. Uncover or bring out the words 'Went immediately'.

2) Unfortunately, the crowds slow them down and, as they press their way through, the woman, also believing Jesus to be the one person who can heal her, touches his cloak. The disciples think he's over-reacting – lots of people would have bumped into him – but Jesus knows this is quite different, a deliberate act of faith, so he stops to find out who it is. He stops what he's doing, if only for a few moments, to care for the person in need. The words here read 'Healed immediately'.

3) The unexpected hold-ups mean Jesus still hasn't reached the child, and by now it's too late. Jairus' friends come out telling him to stop wasting Jesus' time (and possibly his own) because the child's already dead – possibly from an infection such as meningitis which takes hold rapidly. But Jesus won't be put off, and he simply encourages Jairus to hang on to his faith as they head for the house. When they arrive the mourners are in full flow, so Jesus' claim that the girl is just asleep (a euphemism for death) is met with a laugh and jeer. Here reveal the words 'Overcame doubt'.

4) Jesus sends everyone else out of the house, apart from the girl's parents and the three disciples. Once the atmosphere is calmed down he takes them into her room, and holding her hand he tells her to get up. To their amazement she does just that! Jesus didn't want to make a spectacle of the whole thing so he kept this part of his ministry very private, not least out of consideration for both parents and daughter. The words to display now are 'Left doubt outside'.

5) Jesus omits the theology lecture at this point and deals with the most urgent matter – the girl needs food. He also makes the firm request that they say nothing about what's happened, possibly because he knew that otherwise they'd be inundated with attention. This gives the opportunity for the final words, 'Encouraged to live normally'. Even after such an astonishing miracle it wouldn't have been healthy for this little family to think of themselves as something set apart or different. By continuing to live their daily lives fully, they'd automatically be testifying to the power of God to make people whole again.

PROPER 9

Sunday between 3rd and 9th July inclusive

As we move on through the Gospels, in Year A we come now to two passages from Matthew 11 in which the religious leaders' view of Jesus is contrasted with the true perspective. Year B gives Mark's account of the twelve being sent out, which is paralleled by the more detailed version in Luke 10 for Year C – both of these can make use of the outline suggested for Year A of Proper 6.

Hymns

TRADITIONAL

- *All ye who seek a comfort sure*
- *I heard the voice of Jesus say*
- *Lord of all hopefulness*
- *Thy hand, O God, has guided*
- *When I survey the wondrous cross*

MODERN

- *Give thanks with a grateful heart*
- *Great is the Lord and most worthy of praise*
- *I danced in the morning*
- *I, the Lord of sea and sky*
- *Wait for the Lord*

Readings

Year A Genesis 24:34-38, 42-49, 58-67 or
Zechariah 9:9-12; Romans 7:15-25a;
Matthew 11:16-19, 25-30

Year B 2 Samuel 5:1-5, 9-10 or Ezekiel 2:1-5;
2 Corinthians 12:2-10; Mark 6:1-13

Year C 2 Kings 5:1-14 or Isaiah 66:10-14;
Galatians 6:(1-6) 7-16;
Luke 10:1-11, 16-20

Confession

Acknowledging our sinfulness
and trusting in our Saviour,
we confess our sins, saying,
Show us your mercy, O Lord,
and bring us your salvation.

You command us to put no other god
in a higher place than you,
but often we fail to make your kingdom
our top priority.
Show us your mercy, O Lord,
and bring us your salvation.

You command us to love you
with all our heart, soul, mind and strength,
but often our time and energy
is taken up with our own concerns.
Show us your mercy, O Lord,
and bring us your salvation.

You command us to love our neighbours
as ourselves,
but often we are blind to the needs and interests
of those around.
Show us your mercy, O Lord,
and bring us your salvation.

Forgive our failures and wrongdoing,
and give us strength to serve you
with commitment and joy.
Show us your mercy, O Lord,
**and bring us your salvation,
now and in eternity,
through Jesus Christ our Lord. Amen.**

Absolution

Almighty God,
who saves completely those who call upon him,
have mercy on you,
pardon you for every kind of wrong,
and lead you out from darkness
to walk in the light of the Lord,
both now and for ever,
through Christ our Lord. Amen.

Prayer

We enter with joy and thanksgiving
the presence of the Lord who sends us out,
offering to him our prayers and saying,
Lord, as we hear your call,
we will go where you lead.

You send us into this world to bring healing
and the good news of your kingdom.
We pray for areas where suffering and pain
are the everyday experience of so many,
for places clouded by poverty,
inequality and injustice,
and ask you to bless all who seek
to bring them the good news of your love.
Lord, as we hear your call,
we will go where you lead.

You send us into the world together,
to learn to work together
and enjoy partnership in the Gospel.
We pray for the Church,
that a spirit of co-operation
and mutual support
will continue to triumph over barriers
of suspicion and isolationism,
and ask you to bless all Christian ministers,
lay and ordained,
as they lead your people
in proclaiming the good news of your grace.
Lord, as we hear your call,
we will go where you lead.

You send us to the sick and dying,
the despairing and broken-hearted,
to minister your healing touch,
and bring consolation to those
in need of your comfort and peace.
We pray for any known to us,
whether personally or through others,
naming before you . . .
We ask you to bless all who suffer,
and reassure them of the good news
of your risen presence.
Lord, as we hear your call,
we will go where you lead.

You send us out in your name,
not promising that the path will be easy
but with the assurance that your grace
will be sufficient for all our needs.
Lord, as we hear your call,
we will go where you lead,
knowing that you will be with us
until the end of our earthly journey,
and then for evermore.
Accept these prayers in the name
of our Saviour Jesus Christ. Amen.

All-age address

Most of us will say from time to time, 'Whatever I do, it's wrong!', usually implying that we're in a situation where we'll be criticised or condemned, whichever course of action we take. There may be, too, an underlying assumption that those criticising would be determined to find fault under any circumstances. This was certainly true in Jesus' case. Many of his contemporaries had condemned John the Baptist for 'not eating or drinking', but now they were writing Jesus off precisely because he did eat and drink – they'd have refused to see any good in him, no matter what he did. Jesus contrasts this with the attitude of 'little children' a bit later in the chapter. 'Little children' clearly covers more than infants or under-elevens, referring less to an age-group than to a frame of mind, held by people who may not be educated or regard themselves as clever, but who are more open to what God is showing them as a result. This outline therefore looks at ways of learning and perceiving the truth.

1) Those who learn most are those who realise they still have much to learn. Start by asking if anyone's learning French. If someone owns up to studying it for GCSE or A-level, ask them to say a few words. Praise them for their linguistic skills, then produce a French dictionary and ask if they know it from cover to cover. The answer's guaranteed to be 'No', unless the compiler's in the congregation! Go on to say that even if someone knew every single word in the French language, that wouldn't mean they'd know how to write or speak them idiomatically. To do that would also require a comprehensive knowledge of France and its different regions, its history, its culture and so on. Most of us don't know that much about our own country, still less another! Make the point that it would take a pretty daft person to claim they had nothing left to learn. The same is true of the Christian faith – the more we know about God, the Bible and the Christian life, the more we recognise how much we still have to learn.

2) Now ask if anyone's been to another country or even lived there. If possible, get them to describe a few of the differences between that country and your present location. Emphasise that knowing about that country isn't the same as knowing it personally. Even personal knowledge grows throughout our lives, as any happily married couple will attest! Jesus' contemporaries thought they knew everything about God, but as Jesus pointed out on a number of occasions, they didn't know him for themselves. Only in this personal relationship can we experience his gentleness and humility, and his rest when we feel burdened.

3) Finally, half-fill a glass with water and ask someone to describe it. They'll almost certainly say 'half empty' or 'half full'. Then ask two people on opposite sides of the church to say whether it's on their left or right. Of course, both are telling the truth – as they see it! As human beings our perceptions are limited, and we only see things from one point of view. The truth is far greater than we can ever comprehend ourselves, and if the Spirit is to guide us into all truth we must be open to learning and growing as Christians, accepting our limitations and allowing God to teach us his ways.

PROPER 10

Sunday between 10th and 16th July inclusive

This Sunday's readings are all particularly well known. The parable of the sower and its 'explanation' from Matthew 13 forms Year A's Gospel reading; in Year B we have Mark's account of the beheading of John the Baptist; and from Luke 10 in Year C comes arguably the most familiar of all the parables, the Good Samaritan. It's always harder to tackle a very well-known parable, not only to find a rewarding slant on it when Jesus' succinctness speaks for itself, but also because there are plenty of unspoken assumptions around about 'what it really means'. The story of John the Baptist's demise is equally famous, though some may feel its subject matter isn't entirely suitable for an all-age congregation. On the other hand, we should be wary of picking and choosing what we want to read from the Bible, and there's plenty to learn from this sorry sequence of events without dwelling on its more sordid and gory aspects.

Hymns

TRADITIONAL

- *And can it be*
- *Come, ye faithful, raise the anthem*
- *God is working his purpose out*
- *Lord of our life, and God of our salvation*
- *The Lord will come and not be slow*

MODERN

- *I am a new creation*
- *I'm accepted, I'm forgiven*
- *Make way, make way*
- *The Spirit lives to set us free*
- *When I needed a neighbour*

Readings

Year A   Genesis 25:19-34 or Isaiah 55:10-13; Romans 8:1-11; Matthew 13:1-9, 18-23

Year B   2 Samuel 6:1-5, 12b-19 or Amos 7:7-15; Ephesians 1:3-14; Mark 6:14-29

Year C   Amos 7:7-17 or Deuteronomy 30:9-14; Colossians 1:1-14; Luke 10:25-37

Confession

God our Father,
you have commanded us to love you
more than anything else,
and our neighbours as ourselves.
We confess that sometimes we are preoccupied
with the concerns of this world
and fail to give you the highest place in our lives,
that sometimes
we think only of our own needs,
failing to respond to the pain of others.
Have mercy on us, we pray,
forgive our self-centred ways,
and increase our commitment to your kingdom
in lively worship and loving service,
for the sake of your Son, Jesus Christ our Lord.
Amen.

Absolution

Our heavenly Father,
whose care for his children never ceases,
grant you pardon for the wrong you have done
and the good you have not done,
deliver you from self-concern,
and grant you joy in bringing his care
to the world around,
through Christ our Lord. Amen.

Prayer

Together we pray
that the fruits of God's kingdom
may be seen in our lives and in this world
as we say,
Lord, may the seed you sow
bear fruit for your glory.

We ask that the soil of your Church
be productive so that seeds of truth
and righteousness
may grow there for your glory.
Where your people face ill-treatment,
may courage prevail;
where they face corruption,
may truth and integrity overcome;
where they face disinterest,
may your hope and joy triumph.
Lord, may the seed you sow
bear fruit for your glory.

We ask that the soil of society be fruitful
so that seeds of peace and justice
may flourish and prosper.
Where there is violence and conflict,
establish harmony;
where there is poverty and hardship,
transform them with your riches;
where there is despair or misery,
dispel them with your eternal hope.
Lord, may the seed you sow
bear fruit for your glory.

We ask that the barren soil of suffering and pain
be turned into places of growth.
Where there is illness or depression,
give your healing;
where there is loneliness or grief,
give your comfort;
where there is fear or anxiety,
give your encouragement.
Especially we pray for . . .
Lord, may the seed you sow
bear fruit for your glory.

We ask that our own lives may be good soil,
yielding a harvest of goodness and love
for your kingdom.
Lord, may the seed you sow
bear fruit for your glory,
as we hear and respond to your word,
through Jesus Christ our Lord. Amen.

All-age address 1

Jesus' parables are so wonderfully concise, structured and illustrated that any attempt to explain or elaborate them can easily rob them of their power and impact. It's usually best to let them speak for themselves, perhaps with the help of simple visual aids to reinforce the point he's making. The parable of the sower needs nothing more than this, and the only preparation necessary is to gather the relevant items beforehand – a packet of seeds and four large flowerpots: one containing some old rocks or rubble, another with more rocks and rubble lightly covered with soil, one filled with soil and plenty of weeds, and the last one simply holding soil.

1) Take the packet of seeds and read out the instructions which will recommend planting in good clean soil for best results. Open it and display the first flowerpot, asking as you do so whether it will be of any use for these seeds. You should very rapidly get the answer that nothing could grow in it, and any seed that lands on it will be food for birds. Jesus made this same point, and likened it to the people who heard what he said, but immediately forgot about it and carried on as they were before. We still use the expression 'to fall on stony ground' to describe what happens when our words go unheeded. If we fail to listen carefully to God's words, our lives will be like that, completely lifeless, with no personal or spiritual growth.

2) Now bring out the second flowerpot, show it to the congregation, and sprinkle a few seeds on it, again asking what will happen to them. 'Something might grow if you're lucky' is the sort of reply you'll receive. And it might, but not for long or very well. There's enough soil for growth to start but it's too shallow for anything to last, especially in either bad or hot weather. Jesus likened this to people who hear and respond to him, but give up as soon as the going gets tough. Our faith needs to be deeply rooted in him if it's to survive and grow.

3) The third flowerpot is held up for inspection at this point, and again you throw a few seeds on it, in among the weeds, asking how well these might grow. Point out the quantity of soil now available, but add that as long as it's full of weeds they'll strangle the life out of any new plant. Jesus used this to describe those who hear and respond but find their faith choked out by the concerns of everyday life. We need to deal with these distractions by seeing them in their true perspective if our faith is to grow and mature.

4) The final pot should meet with everyone's approval for planting seeds! This soil will be productive because it's clean, rich and deep enough for plants to grow and develop. Conclude by saying that if we're to grow as Christians and become mature in our faith, we need to sort out the parts of our lives which are stony, shallow or weed-ridden.

Sometimes we hear God's voice but it makes no impression at all; sometimes we start to respond but it soon seems too hard and we give up; sometimes we mean to respond to him, but become distracted by concerns here and now. Jesus wants us to be fruitful for him, like the good soil, so that our lives demonstrate the good news of his love and care, and so that our trust in him becomes deeper as we go through life.

All-age address 2

It's said that there have been more Christian martyrs in the twentieth century than in the previous nineteen since the time of Christ. There's no reason to doubt this statistic, but most Christians in western society won't have first-hand experience of facing ill-treatment or even death for their faith. The worst we're likely to endure is a bit of ridicule or 'cold shouldering'. This outline develops the idea of suffering for one's faith from the story of John the Baptist.

1) Gather together a few symbols of punishment – a cane or strap, a detention book from school, handcuffs, etc. Alternatively, draw them on an OHP transparency, and as you reveal them ask what sort of offence these might punish – for example, being cheeky to parents, failing to do homework, stealing. (Many parents have given up using the smack as a corrective and some may be offended by the suggestion that it's a suitable way to reprimand bad behaviour, so you may wish to consider how you express this, even though you're talking in general terms.) Point out that there are different punishments designed to reflect the severity of the offence, from a ticking-off to imprisonment. But we all recognise the injustice of someone receiving a punishment when they've done no wrong. That's what had happened to John the Baptist. He'd been imprisoned for questioning King Herod's personal life and pointing out its shortcomings.

2) Now say that John had suffered for two reasons – he'd stood up for the right way to

behave, and confronted someone powerful who was disobeying God's law. Herod himself was intrigued by John, but his new wife was infuriated and wanted him dead. Herod was a weak man, and in a vulnerable moment he allowed himself to be manipulated into executing John. Explain that while we probably won't be imprisoned for our faith, we may suffer in other ways. If possible, OHP drawings will help to reinforce the following points:

a) We may well be laughed at (for going to church, for not doing something wrong).

b) We may lose friends (especially if they feel threatened by our faith).

c) We may miss out on promotion or other opportunities because we won't behave dishonestly or tread on other people.

d) We may feel very vulnerable, especially with those who have authority over us.

John must have known what might happen to him for speaking out but he was courageous enough not to give in to fear and compromise himself. Many Christians have suffered similarly since then. The deeper our faith is, the stronger we'll be when such a time of testing comes our way.

All-age address 3

So familiar is the story of the Good Samaritan, that the term is often used to refer to any act of kindness out of the ordinary. What we lose is the sense of just how radical Jesus' words were to his contemporaries, since Samaritans and Jews were as far apart then, socially and religiously, as Ulster Catholics and Protestants, or Jews and Palestinians today. The lawyer who asked the question thought he'd found a clever way to trap Jesus, but he soon found himself on the back foot, and tried to escape by asking for a definition of 'neighbour' – maybe he regretted it later!

This outline is built around Jesus' redefinition of who our neighbour is, and his challenge to some of our deeply-held prejudices. It needs a couple of willing volunteers to act as victims.

1) The first person staggers into the church with torn clothes, tousled hair, and, if possible,

'wounds' created by make-up or face-paint – a small amount of tomato ketchup will also add to the realism! – and collapses, in full view of the congregation. There may be a general reaction of surprise at this, so first ask who'd be willing to help the victim – one or two may well offer. Follow this up with a question about whether they'd still be willing to do so if they knew the man was a terrorist, or an AIDS patient, or perhaps someone they'd fallen out with and weren't speaking to. Point out that it's easy to make a good impression when the circumstances are right, but generally it's much easier to make an excuse not to get our hands dirty, as the priest and the lawyer did in Jesus' parable. This man needed immediate practical help, and he received it, not from those who'd have been expected to demonstrate God's love, but from a Samaritan who they'd have despised. Being a neighbour means interrupting what we're doing, however important it may seem, to help someone in need, rather than trying to justify our non-involvement.

2) The second volunteer comes in dressed as a tramp, shaking an old cap with a few coins in it. Again ask how many would be willing to help this person (though you could stress that money isn't necessarily the best help to give as it might be used for harmful purposes). It's easy to be judgemental about such people, but Jesus doesn't allow for that. The Samaritan doesn't ask about the victim's cultural or educational background, his religious beliefs, or even his personal circumstances. Our excuses are usually ways of disguising these man-made barriers, but in God's kingdom they have no place. The lawyer who asked the question found it thrown back at him – which one is the true neighbour? The answer was clear enough, and so was Jesus' reply, 'Go and do likewise', which applies to us as much as to those who heard Jesus at the time.

PROPER 11

Sunday between 17th and 23rd July inclusive

The parable of the weeds forms the extract from Matthew's Gospel in Year A, continuing the kingdom parables from chapter 13. Year B gives us two extracts from Mark 6, which form the start of his account of the feeding of the five thousand and its sequel, while in Year C we have Luke's brief narrative of a homely scene chez Martha and Mary. A suitable outline address for both Years B and C can be found at Proper 1, contrasting the need to be active for God's kingdom with the need for rest and refreshment, growing and learning.

Hymns

TRADITIONAL

- *Alleluia, alleluia, hearts to heaven and voices raise*
- *At the name of Jesus*
- *In heavenly love abiding*
- *The King of love my shepherd is*
- *Come, risen Lord, and deign to be our guest*

MODERN

- *Abba, Father, let me be*
- *Gather around, for the table is spread*
- *Jesus, stand among us at the meeting of our lives*
- *Wait for the Lord, whose day is near*
- *You are beautiful*

Readings

Year A   Genesis 28:10-19a or Isaiah 44:6-8;
Romans 8:12-25;
Matthew 13:24-30, 36-43

Year B   2 Samuel 7:1-14a or Jeremiah 23:1-6;
Ephesians 2:11-22; Mark 6:30-34, 53-56

Year C   Amos 8:1-12 or Genesis 18:1-10a;
Colossians 1:15-28; Luke 10:38-42

Confession

Father of all,
we confess to you our sin and wrongdoing,
and ask your forgiveness
for the times when we have failed you.
For allowing the pressures of everyday life
to crowd you out,
for giving in to temptation's subtle voice,
and for not responding to your loving call,
pardon and deliver us, we pray.
Give us strength to resist
the easy path to destruction,
and to follow the route of Christ
which leads to life eternal,
in whose name we ask this. Amen.

Absolution

Almighty God,
the source of all life and love,
have mercy on you,
forgive all your sins and failings,
and by his Spirit enable you
to overcome evil and live for him,
through our Saviour Jesus Christ. Amen.

Prayer

We come to our heavenly Father,
finding it difficult
to put our deepest thoughts into words,
but knowing his Spirit will help us.
Lord, hear the cry of our hearts,
and show us how to pray.

We are often confused and disturbed
by events in the world around us.
Crime, cruelty, abuse and neglect
wreck many lives;
dishonesty and greed disfigure public life;
suffering and hardship go unnoticed
and untouched.
By your Spirit guide those
who have authority and influence
in the paths of right,
and give hope to the vulnerable and needy.
Lord, hear the cry of our hearts,
and show us how to pray.

Sometimes we are distressed
by conflicts and discord in the Church.
Disagreements turn into rifts;
human differences become barriers;
fellowship and unity splinter apart.
Bless all Christian leaders and teachers,
and by your Spirit enable your people
to overcome obstacles
and work together in your service.
Lord, hear the cry of our hearts,
and show us how to pray.

We share in the sadness of those we know
who are enduring times of pain and distress.
We pray for those whose lives are diminished
by illness, immobility, anxiety or desolation,
especially . . .
Comfort and heal those we are concerned for,
and bring them through all their troubles.
Lord, hear the cry of our hearts,
and show us how to pray.

Be with us in pleasure and perplexity,
and lead us in the ways of eternal life,
that we may rejoice in the hope
you set before us
and live confidently for your glory.
Lord, hear the cry of our hearts,
and show us how to pray,
as we live day by day
in the power of your Spirit,
through Jesus Christ our Lord. Amen.

All-age address

The parable of the wheat and the tares raises
the thorny issue of God being our judge, a
concept our society doesn't find easy to
accept. Yet at the same time judgementalism
is rife, as the media demonstrate endlessly.
However, it's important to avoid the trap of
suggesting that God shares our judgements
and makes all the same choices as we do. So
this outline looks at the sort of choices we
make, how we make them, and how God's
judgements differ from that. Some preparation
is necessary so that those who volunteer are
able to make their choices, but this can be as
basic or elaborate as time and circumstances
allow. As always, care is needed if the illustration isn't to overrun the points it's reinforcing.

1) Offer a selection of three types of confec-
   tionery – for example, a toffee, a chocolate
   and a wine gum – and ask someone to come
   up and choose one. When they've done so,
   ask them why they made that particular
   choice. Taste, colour and texture will all
   play a part, as might childhood memories,
   but the grounds given will be personal and
   entirely arbitrary – indeed, on another
   occasion the same person might well
   choose differently! It's very important to
   stress that, unlike this, God doesn't judge
   us in a subjective or arbitrary way.

2) Next hold up three ties of very different
   colours and design, and ask another volunteer to come and select one. Although this
   will also be somewhat random, another
   criterion comes into play, namely the
   circumstances in which the tie will be used
   – a funeral, a wedding, a business meeting,
   a party perhaps. Explain that God doesn't
   judge people according to whether they
   suit his purposes, and write off those
   who don't.

3) Find three reasonably large pictures of
   well-known footballers (the sport isn't
   important, but football probably has the
   broadest range of appeal), and paste them
   on to card (you may find your local team
   has publicity shots they'll let you have). As
   you exhibit them, ask which one should
   be playing for England (Wales, Scotland,
   Ireland, or whatever team is relevant locally).
   No doubt you'll get a variety of views
   offered, all based on some kind of reasoning
   – one person may think a strong defender is
   necessary, to prevent goals being given
   away, another will prefer a midfielder who
   can win the ball, or a striker who can score
   a lot of goals. However, God doesn't judge
   us according to our ability. Instead he
   chooses us and gives us the gifts we need to
   serve and obey him, and the strength to live
   by faith.

4) Finally, bring out three wedding photos,
   asking as you do so why these people chose
   each other. It's unlikely that anyone would
   choose a life partner on the basis of their
   ability, or because they fit a particular
   purpose, yet neither would they say their
   decision was arbitrary. The overriding factor
   in choosing a spouse is love. Conclude by
   emphasising that God chooses us, too,
   because he loves us. Jesus' parable contrasts
   the servants' attitude with the owner's. They
   wanted to root out the weeds immediately
   (just as we like immediate judgements), but
   the owner tells them to wait until the harvest
   is finally ready to be gathered; otherwise
   they'll risk destroying some of the wheat as
   well. We can't make judgements on God's
   behalf, but we can be sure that, unlike ours,
   his will always be fair.

PROPER 12

Sunday between 24th and 30th July inclusive

This Sunday, the Year A reading from Matthew concludes the kingdom parables from chapter 13, while Year C gives us Luke's account of the Lord's Prayer and Jesus' teaching on prayer. However, Year B diverts us for a few weeks into John's Gospel, with a sequence of readings from chapter 6. The first of these covers the feeding of the five thousand, picking up from the section omitted last week in Mark 6.

Hymns

TRADITIONAL

- *Eternal Father, strong to save*
- *Jesu, priceless treasure*
- *Just as I am, without one plea*
- *Lord, teach us how to pray aright*
- *Thy kingdom come, O God*

MODERN

- *Do not be afraid*
- *I give you all the honour*
- *O Lord, hear my prayer*
- *Our Father, who art in heaven*
- *Seek ye first*

Readings

Year A   Genesis 29:15-28 or 1 Kings 3:5-12;
          Romans 8:26-39;
          Matthew 13:31-33, 44-52
Year B   2 Samuel 11:1-15 or 2 Kings 4:42-44;
          Ephesians 3:14-21; John 6:1-21
Year C   Hosea 1:2-10 or Genesis 18:20-32;
          Colossians 2:6-15 (16-19); Luke 11:1-13

Confession

We reach out to the Lord our God,
who is merciful and forgiving,
even though we have rebelled
against him, saying,
we turn to you in repentance;
Lord, pardon and restore us.

For pursuing our own ends,
instead of obeying your will,
we turn to you in repentance;
Lord, pardon and restore us.

For seeking human acclaim,
instead of waiting for your 'Well done!',
we turn to you in repentance;
Lord, pardon and restore us.

For putting our faith in this passing world,
instead of trusting your eternal love,
we turn to you in repentance;
Lord, pardon and restore us.

For behaving as though you did not matter,
instead of owning you as our King,
we turn to you in repentance;
**Lord, pardon and restore us,
and make us fit for your service
through Christ our Saviour. Amen.**

Absolution

God, who is slow to anger and swift to bless,
forgive all your sins and wrongdoing,
give you strength to obey him,
and fill you with the joy of his eternal kingdom,
through Jesus Christ our Lord. Amen.

Prayer

We come with confidence to God our Father,
praying as he teaches
for his kingdom to come and his will to be done.
Lord, we ask this in your name;
hear us as we pray in faith.

May your will be done in the world around us,
spoiled and degraded by our unwillingness
to act as good stewards of its riches.
Help us to care for your creation
and to work so that all people may share
in what your goodness has provided.
Lord, we ask this in your name;
hear us as we pray in faith.

May your will be done
through governments and leaders,
as they lead the nations of the world
in peace and conflict, prosperity and adversity.

Help them to count the common good
above personal ambition,
to resist the temptations of power
and to promote justice
and equality for all people.
Lord, we ask this in your name;
hear us as we pray in faith.

May your will be done in our local community,
through the work of councillors
and care organisations.
Help schools to nurture the children in their care
in your ways;
social workers to provide new directions
in the lives of the needy and vulnerable;
surgeries and hospitals to give relief
and healing for the sick in body and mind;
hospices and retirement homes
to bring comfort and hope
to those nearing the end of their lives.
Lord, we ask this in your name;
hear us as we pray in faith.

May your will be done
in the lives of those we know
who need your comfort and healing,
especially . . .
Help them to know you
alongside them in their troubles,
and pierce the dark clouds
of their present difficulties
with the light of your eternal presence.
Lord, we ask this in your name;
hear us as we pray in faith.

May your will be done through us
as we worship and serve you.
Help us to be channels of your peace
wherever we are,
and to bring your light
into the darkness of our world.
Lord, we ask this in your name;
**hear us as we pray in faith
for the sake of your Son,
our Lord Jesus Christ. Amen.**

All-age address 1

So far the Gospel readings from Matthew 13
have covered just two parables – the sower
and the weeds. Today's verses cover another

five! However, they're very brief, with just one
(the net) returning to the theme of judgement,
and the others focusing more on growth,
impact and value. At first a mustard seed, a
lump of yeast and a hidden pearl seem to have
little in common, but in Jesus' parables all start
off insignificant or hidden; only later are they
seen to increase beyond imagining in scope,
effect and value. The props for this outline are
basic and should prove easy to obtain.

1) Take a fairly small seed (preferably one that
   can be seen only at close quarters) and
   place it in an unmarked envelope prior to
   the service. As you start, take it out and ask
   if someone can identify it. One or two
   might think it's a speck of dust, others will
   guess correctly that it'll grow into something
   if planted – an expert gardener might even
   identify it correctly! At a suitable point, tell
   the congregation what the seed will grow
   into when it's planted. It may not be at all
   obvious now, but it contains all that's
   necessary in the right growing conditions
   to become a geranium, lettuce or whatever
   you've chosen. The seed of God's kingdom
   will also grow so that, while it may seem
   very insignificant now, in due course it will
   come to dominate everything else.

2) Instead of putting live yeast into bread
   dough (rather messy as part of the liturgy!)
   a simpler way of conveying Jesus' second
   point is to make a cup of tea or coffee,
   and ask someone to add milk and sugar.
   Then suggest they drink without either –
   which they'll immediately say is impossible.
   Like the yeast in Jesus' parable, the sugar
   and milk permeate the whole drink and
   change its taste permanently. God's kingdom
   may seem as small as those grains of sugar
   or a dash of milk, but one day it will come
   to influence the whole world.

3) The final picture is of something valuable but
   hidden, so that its value is only recognised
   by a few. Try to find something of moderate
   value which has been stored in the loft for
   some years, or discovered in a junk shop,
   without anyone realising its true worth – an
   old piece of jewellery or piece of porcelain
   might fit the bill, although an old Dinky car

is also an excellent example as its value is less immediately obvious. You could ask the congregation to suggest how much the article is worth, but then add that it's not for sale because it's valuable to you. We treasure our own special possessions but Jesus wants his followers to put an even higher value on his kingdom, so that we'd be willing to give up almost anything else to obtain it. Conclude by reiterating Jesus' final point, that the kingdom's treasures are both old and new, to be found both in the wisdom of the past and the insights of the present.

All-age address 2

The narrative of the feeding of the five thousand, in John's Gospel at least, has a distinctly eucharistic flavour which is brought out more fully towards the end of this chapter. This outline therefore concentrates more on the parable itself and the importance of being fed spiritually as well as physically. A variety of foods will need to be brought in to illustrate the parallels.

1) Carbohydrates are well-illustrated by a bread roll, potato or bowl of cereal. Most people are now well clued up about dietary matters (not least children from their school lessons), so it should be easy to extract the information that such foods are vital as a source of energy and warmth.

2) Proteins could be represented by milk or an egg, and somebody is likely to know that they're particularly useful for promoting the body's healing function, as well as providing more energy and heat!

3) Eggs exemplify the fats (as do cheese and butter). They too produce energy and warmth, but also help particular organs to work correctly, such as kidneys and eyes.

4) Vitamins can also be found in dairy products, though an orange or banana would serve equally well. Everybody knows they're necessary to maintain the body in good working order, and to assist in the production of antibodies which fight disease.

5) Minerals such as calcium, found in dairy produce and green vegetables, are vital for healthy bones and teeth, while iron (in eggs, green vegetables and wholemeal bread) is essential for the blood.

6) Roughage is found in most vegetables and fruits (as well as cereals and certain types of bread), and is vital if the appetite is to be satisfied.

Don't allow this to degenerate into a science lesson – the point is that we all need a diet which contains these good things if we're to be healthy and well. Parallel each of these with the spiritual nourishment we need if we're to be truly whole. God's word gives strength and vitality of spirit to those who receive it; it promotes healing and wholeness; it's as essential to our daily living and health as good food; it satisfies us in the way nothing else can. No doctor would suggest we have anything other than a healthy diet. As Christians we must give our spiritual diet an equally high priority.

All-age address 3

Jesus' teaching on prayer has never been equalled for its depth and richness, nor for its utter simplicity. Any attempt to be too elaborate or glib in handling the subject is bound to miss the target, so this outline aims simply to open up the significance for ourselves of Jesus' words to his disciples – that if they ask they will receive, if they seek they will find, if they knock there'll be a reply. Preparation involves making three cards, each written on both sides. The first has 'Ask' with 'Receive' on its reverse; the second has 'Seek' backed by 'Find'; the third has 'Knock' on one side and 'Open' on the other.

1) Start by asking what various members of the congregation would like as a birthday present (adding that you're not making any promises!). Some will make very modest demands, but others will be hoping for a new bicycle, computer, clothes, even a car. Point out that while asking for something is legitimate, there's no obligation on the donor to provide it! Ask a volunteer to hold

up the 'Ask' card at this point. Children will ask for all sorts of gifts, but for most families there isn't enough money to buy everything that's asked for, and wise parents or guardians recognise that, however much money they may have, it would be bad for children to be given whatever they want. Jesus certainly wasn't suggesting that his heavenly Father would give us absolutely anything – we'd all like more money, or a bigger house, but we'd soon become selfish and materialistic if God only answered prayers like those. Instead, Jesus wants us to keep on praying for things God wants, for his kingdom to come and for his will to be done, not least through us. Turn the card round now, and stress that if we pray like this we'll always receive an answer from God, even if it isn't the one we thought we'd get.

2) Display the 'Seek' card next, and ask if anyone's lost anything recently – the chances are that you'll hear about keys, credit cards, umbrellas or handbags! It's likely that someone will be willing to say how they tried to find the lost article. Maybe they turned the house out, returned to where they'd been earlier, or even phoned the police. If we lose something valuable we'll go to any lengths to find it again. God's kingdom's like that – (reverse the card as you make this point). The more effort we put into seeking his will, the more blessing we'll find in doing it.

3) Finally have someone hold up the 'Knock' card. Ask who enjoys visiting friends, and then whether their friends are always in when they call. If we know someone's in the house, especially if they've invited us, we'll carry on knocking at the door (in a polite British way, of course!) until the door is opened. Now reverse the card, saying finally that if we're faithful in our praying, God will open the door of opportunity at exactly the right time for us. It won't be an opportunity to serve our own ends, but to build God's kingdom and serve him.

Proper 13

Sunday between 31st July and 6th August inclusive

For Year A Matthew's Gospel provides us this week with his account of the feeding of the five thousand, while in Year B Mark continues to be replaced by chapter 6 of John's Gospel. As we continue with Luke in Year C he records Jesus' parable of the rich fool, a passage which resonates deeply with our own times. A suitable outline address for Year A can be found under Proper 12.

Hymns

TRADITIONAL

- *Alleluia, sing to Jesus*
- *Guide me, O thou great Redeemer*
- *Now is eternal life*
- *Praise, my soul, the King of heaven*
- *Take my life, and let it be*

MODERN

- *All that I am*
- *Bread is blessed and broken*
- *I am the bread of life*
- *Let us praise God together*
- *My Lord, what love is this*

Readings

Year A Genesis 32:22-31 or Isaiah 55:1-5; Romans 9:1-5; Matthew 14:13-21
Year B 2 Samuel 11:26-12:13a or Exodus 16:2-4, 9-15; Ephesians 4:1-16; John 6:24-35
Year C Hosea 11:1-11 or Ecclesiastes 1:2, 12-14; 2:18-23; Colossians 3:1-11; Luke 12:13-21

Confession

We kneel before you, Creator God,
in penitence and sorrow
for our many failures.
We have used your world
to accumulate personal wealth
rather than build your kingdom;
we have put personal comfort
above meeting the needs of others;
we have lived according to human wisdom
rather than by faith in you.
Have mercy on us, we pray,
forgive our self-centredness,
and by your Spirit help us
to store up treasure in heaven,
for the sake of your Son,
our Saviour Jesus Christ. Amen.

Absolution

Almighty God,
who has made all things for our enjoyment,
grant you forgiveness for all your sins,
and strength to live a new life by faith in him,
fixing your eyes on the things which are above,
through Christ our Lord. Amen.

Prayer

Our heavenly Father,
who created the whole vast universe,
knows our every need
and the inexpressible prayers of our hearts,
which we bring to him now, saying,
Lord, we call on you for you will answer;
give ear to us and hear our prayer.

Hear us as we pray for our Church
and those who lead it,
both locally and nationally,
especially . . .
Bless and guide the work of all Christian leaders,
evangelists and mission workers,
pastors and teachers, prophets and preachers,
that their ministry may build up
the Body of Christ
enabling us to work together
to bring other people into your kingdom.
Lord, we call on you for you will answer;
give ear to us and hear our prayer.

Hear us as we pray for this world
and those you have given authority over it,
in this country and elsewhere, especially . . .
Bless and guide the decisions and actions
of all politicians and governments,
bankers and economists,
that they may strive for peace and justice

and a fair distribution of the resources
you have given to all people.
Lord, we call on you for you will answer;
give ear to us and hear our prayer.

Hear us as we pray for the needy and deprived:
for those who have no home
or family,
those who are vulnerable
and open to exploitation
or abuse by the powerful,
those who lack the most basic
requirements for living,
and especially . . .
Bless and guide all who work
to relieve suffering and hardship
that your compassion may be seen in them.
Lord, we call on you for you will answer;
give ear to us and hear our prayer.

Hear us as we pray
for our own loved ones and neighbours,
those passing through the dark shadows
of suffering and pain of mind or body,
especially . . .
Bless and guide them in their times of distress
hide them in the shadow of your wings.
Lord, we call on you for you will answer;
give ear to us and hear our prayer.

Hear us as we pray for ourselves,
that our steps may hold to your paths
as we walk with you by faith.
Lord, we call on you for you will answer;
give ear to us and hear our prayer,
for the sake of your Son,
our Saviour Jesus Christ. Amen.

All-age address 1

For something which forms a staple part of
our diet, bread comes in an incredible variety
of forms. Apart from the sliced loaves which
come in packets, we can buy cottage or wholemeal loaves, bloomers or baguettes, split tins
or ciabatti, rye bread, pittas, nans . . . and as
well as their nutritional value they make a
very attractive illustration for an all-age talk!
This outline develops the idea of Jesus as the
Bread of Life, using the real thing to help us
understand something of what he meant. A

few examples of different types of bread are
needed (including one or two of foreign origin),
and, if possible, a lump of bread dough, some
yeast, and 'one you prepared earlier'. You may
find an enthusiastic baker among the congregation to help you with the latter, but bear in
mind that this is slightly messy and requires
an apron to ensure clothes aren't spoiled. If
you normally wear robes, you may feel they're
not the most suitable attire!

1) First bring out the dough and either ask for
a volunteer to come and knead it or do so
yourself. At the same time, ask why bread
is so important in our diet. There are
several possible responses to this, the first of
which is likely to be 'It's good for us'. Bread
contains many elements which promote
good health, though it's not necessary to
list them. Just as bread forms the basis of
our diet, so we also need Jesus to be our
spiritual diet. Listening to him, following
him, growing in him, are all essential to our
spiritual health.

2) The next response may well be 'You can use
it for anything'. Bread is very adaptable, can
be used in a variety of ways and blends well
with most other tastes. There's no situation
in life in which Jesus doesn't fit, because all
life has its origin in him. His presence
transforms even the bleakest of outlooks.

3) Another possible response is 'It fills you
up' – you may get this from mothers who
have to feed hungry offspring! A couple of
rounds of sandwiches doesn't leave a lot of
room for anything else. Just as bread can
satisfy our physical hunger, so Jesus, the
Bread of Life, satisfies our spiritual hunger
or longing. As we feed on him day by day
we find that we need nothing else.

4) If you're using dough and yeast, bring out
the yeast at this point and explain that the
bread won't rise without it. Add some yeast
and ask why it isn't rising, then explain that
the yeast needs time to work through the
whole lump of dough. The same is true of
our spiritual life – it doesn't just suddenly
happen but, like the yeast, God's love
gradually affects the whole way we think

and live, which you can demonstrate by bringing out a baked loaf that's ready to eat.

5) Finally display a few different kinds of bread from across the world, at the same time emphasising that Jesus is the Bread of Life for all people, whatever their colour, race, education, age or gender.

All-age address 2

Jesus wasn't one to pull his punches, and throughout the Gospels he regularly challenges the assumptions of the day, not least in practical matters such as money. This parable was his response to a rather tedious question from someone who wanted to prove he was in the right in a dispute with his brother over a legacy. Jesus refused to be drawn into taking sides, but he also got under his questioner's skin by confronting his need to increase his wealth. The parable of the rich man who thought he'd got it made is a chilling indictment of this mentality – in this world's terms he appeared successful and well-heeled, but in God's eyes he was a short-sighted fool who was prepared to mortgage his eternal future for what proved to be very short-term gain. We too live in a society which confuses making the most of each moment as a gift from God with living for the moment, as though there were no future. This outline aims to address, as Jesus did, the prevailing short-term materialistic philosophy by which many people live, and requires just a few simple preparations plus a couple of forewarned volunteers.

1) Find an old print or painting which is of little or no value and describe it as though you were an expert on the Antiques Roadshow. Make it clear that you've found this in the loft and you're convinced it's a priceless old master which will make you a fortune! You could even say how you'd use the hundreds of thousands of pounds it must be worth. Then go to your first volunteer, who poses as an art expert and explains that the most he could offer you for it is £2.46. Express your disappointment, but go on to indicate that even if it had been worth a vast sum, you wouldn't have been any

happier. In fact, many of those who've won huge sums on the Lottery have become miserable as a result. Jesus wanted the man to realise that while we need money to live, if it takes over our life we'll become discontented and unhappy.

2) Prepare a piece of paper on which is written 'Share Certificate' and '1,000,000'. If it looks authentic so much the better, though nobody will be fooled. Tell everyone that your investments have paid off and you've got a million shares, so you're going to the bank manager to cash them. Your second volunteer acts this role, and tells you that the companies you've invested in have gone bankrupt, so the shares are worthless. After a brief show of disappointment explain that during the Black Monday share crash of 1987 many people who thought they'd got rich quickly suddenly discovered they had nothing. The wealth of this world is very short-lived, and can't bring any lasting satisfaction. Jesus wanted his hearers to understand that the best investment they could ever make was in God's kingdom. The gains aren't immediate or spectacular, but they last for ever.

3) Jesus finishes his parable with the rich man's death. All his wealth will go to someone else and he'll soon be forgotten, because he was interested only in feathering his own nest. By making God's kingdom our priority we get the 'treasures' of this world in their proper perspective, to be enjoyed, but above all used for God's glory and to bring his love and care to others, especially those in need. All of us have to die and then answer to God for what we did with our lives. Since we don't know when that will be, how important it is to be prepared for it now.

PROPER 14

Sunday between 7th and 13th August inclusive

We continue in Matthew 14 in Year A with his account of Jesus walking on water, to which the writer adds how Peter attempted to emulate this – the outline suggested in Proper 7 for Year C could be used for this, though a brief addition is added here to tackle Peter's failure to walk on the lake. In Year B we have a third extract from Jesus' Bread of Life discourse in John 6, and in Year C Luke's Gospel continues in chapter 12 with more of Jesus' teaching about wealth and 'investing our treasure' in heaven, including the parable of the servants who were ready for their master's return.

Hymns

TRADITIONAL

- *Jesu, thou joy of loving hearts*
- *Lord, enthroned in heavenly splendour*
- *O God, our help in ages past*
- *We hail thy presence glorious*
- *Ye servants of the Lord*

MODERN

- *Come on and celebrate*
- *Great is the Lord*
- *God is good, we sing and shout it*
- *Nada te turbe*
- *Only by grace can we enter*

Readings

Year A   Genesis 37:1-4, 12-28 or
1 Kings 19:9-18; Romans 10:5-15;
Matthew 14:22-33
Year B   2 Samuel 18:5-9, 15, 31-33 or
1 Kings 19:4-8; Ephesians 4:25-5:2;
John 6:35, 41-51
Year C   Isaiah 1:1, 10-20 or Genesis 15:1-6;
Hebrews 11:1-3, 8-16; Luke 12:32-40

Confession

We turn back to the Lord,
from whose paths we have strayed, saying,
In your mercy, O Lord,
redeem us and help us.

You created our hands for loving service,
but we have used them to grasp and snatch.
In your mercy, O Lord,
redeem us and help us.

You created our lips to sing your praise
and tell your good news,
but we have used them to criticise and scorn.
In your mercy, O Lord,
redeem us and help us.

You created our minds to think of your glory,
but we have dwelt only on this passing world.
In your mercy, O Lord,
redeem us and help us.

You created our hearts to respond to your love
and share it with others,
but we have considered only our own interests.
In your mercy, O Lord,
redeem us and help us.
to live the new life
in Jesus Christ our Lord. Amen.

Absolution

Almighty God,
who created you in his own image,
forgive your waywardness and sinfulness,
pardon your wrongdoing,
and restore you to himself through his Son,
Jesus Christ our Lord. Amen.

Prayer

In confidence and with quiet hearts
we approach our heavenly Father
with our prayers and thanksgiving, saying,
Lord, our hope is in you;
with you there is unfailing love.

We bring you our concerns
for the many hurting places of our world,
where poverty and starvation,
hatred and conflict
deprive people of security and freedom.
Especially we pray for . . .
We pray too for those
whose pain is continuous –
the homeless, drug addicts, alcoholics,
the isolated, and victims of abuse.
May the distress in our hearts
turn into practical action
to share your love with them.

Lord, our hope is in you;
with you there is unfailing love.

We bring you our prayers for the Church –
for our local fellowship and ecumenical groups
in this community,
for Christian leaders, both local and national,
and for your people throughout the world.
We pray too for all projects and initiatives
which aim to bring your people together
and demonstrate the good news of Jesus
to those who do not know it.
Lord, our hope is in you;
with you there is unfailing love.

We bring you our loved ones and friends,
and those in our community who are burdened
with care or suffering, especially . . .
We pray too for carers, counsellors,
doctors and other medical staff,
whose work is to bring relief and healing.
Lord, our hope is in you;
with you there is unfailing love.

We bring you those who have died
in the faith of Christ, especially . . .
asking that we may be challenged
by their example
and encouraged by their commitment.
We pray too for those enduring
the lonely grief of bereavement,
and ask you to bless and comfort them.
Lord, our hope is in you;
with you there is unfailing love.

Heavenly Father,
we bring you ourselves,
weak and fallible though we are,
and pray for the strength and guidance
of the Holy Spirit to help us live for you.
Lord, our hope is in you;
**with you there is unfailing love,
seen in your Son Jesus Christ,
through whom we offer these prayers. Amen.**

All-age address 1

The second outline address for Proper 7 (based
on Mark's account of Jesus calming the storm)
is equally applicable to Matthew's account.
However, Matthew adds the extra dimension
of Peter's attempt to walk on the water, so you
might prefer to use this adaptation of the third
point.

Start by showing the picture of a round-the-
world voyage (or some similar achievement)
and talk briefly about the natural fear the
participants must have had, and how they
prepared thoroughly for every possible risk
and eventuality. Peter wasn't trying to achieve
something he'd been working up to for most
of his life. He wanted Jesus to prove who he
really was by giving him the courage to walk
on the water. But his fear got the better of his
faith, and Jesus had to catch hold of him as he
started to sink in the wind-driven waves. We'd
probably all share Peter's terror in this situation,
but the power of Jesus can overcome even our
deepest human fears if we allow him to be
Lord of our lives as well as Lord of creation.

All-age address 2

The more extended discourses and passages of
John's Gospel require rather more thought if
they're to be translated effectively and mean-
ingfully into an all-age worship address. In
this section of chapter 6 Jesus' statement that he
is the Bread of Life has irritated the religious
leadership, who cope with it by belittling his
background and trying to make him merely
human. All they could see was the carpenter's
son from Nazareth, so they were blind to the
bigger picture. This outline is simple, but a
little preparation is necessary. Take a couple of
full-page pictures from the ever-useful Sunday
colour supplements (or any other source, provided the picture is at least A4 size and easily
recognised). One should be of a well-known
person (ideally a pop star, TV or sporting
personality who children will relate to); the
other could be of a well-known place (Nelson's
Column, Tower Bridge, the Eiffel Tower, or
anywhere else the congregation will identify
straightaway). Paste them on to card and cut
them into five or six irregular-shaped pieces.

1) Take the first picture (it doesn't matter which)
and show the congregation one piece of it.
Ask if anyone knows who or where it is –
ideally any guesses will be wrong at this
stage! Add a piece at a time, stopping to ask
if anyone's worked it out. Sooner or later it
will become obvious. Explain that often we
don't recognise things because we only see
one part of the picture. That was the

religious leaders' problem. All they saw was a carpenter's son, and they got it wrong because they wouldn't look any further.

2) Now go through the same process with the second picture. This time explain that the people of Jesus' time didn't know all that we now do, and they hadn't yet recognised the connection between the manna in the wilderness (a story they'd have all learned as children) and Jesus who said he was the bread who came down from heaven. Only later did the early Christians recognise what he really meant as they celebrated the 'Lord's Supper' as Jesus had commanded them. They knew who Jesus was, and slowly their eyes were opened to see how the whole of his life made sense in the light of their scriptures, the Old Testament. Conclude by emphasising how easy it is for all of us to reduce Jesus down to one small part of the picture and ignore everything else. Stress the importance of us having open eyes so that we see the 'big picture', and understand Jesus not just in terms of the whole Bible, essential though that is, but in the context of our own lives too, and the lives of other people.

All-age address 3

Jesus often spoke of the need for his followers to be ready – something we thought about at Advent. The passage from Luke's Gospel combines the parable of the reliable servants who were ready for their master's return with the action required of us to ensure that we're similarly ready. A suitable outline address can be found in Book 1 of *Come to the Feast* (all-age address 2 for Advent Sunday), but the following is an adaptation of that. It needs a couple of primed volunteers and a few props – a couple of dusters and some furniture polish, some flowers in a vase, and some token dinner-party food (a bottle of wine, a few 'nibbles' and maybe a couple of glasses). You could also use a table and chairs as the 'set' for a room, though this isn't necessary.

1) Your volunteers are hosts expecting some guests, although there's some uncertainty about their arrival time. Indicate that they want to be properly ready whenever this should be, so they're making preparations. The first volunteer is busy with the duster and polish, and when you ask what they're up to, they should explain that 'the place is a tip', and in need of a clean and tidy-up. If we invite guests to our home we want it to look clean and presentable, rather than dusty, grubby, and littered with old newspapers or sweet wrappers. If we're to be ready for Jesus, our master, our lives need to be cleaned up, and all the clutter and mess sorted out. That's not something we can do by ourselves, so we need his strength and forgiveness to enable us to deal with it.

2) The second volunteer starts to arrange the glasses and brings out the wine and nibbles (or whatever's appropriate to your community). When you ask why they're doing this, they say that it's much easier to pay attention to guests if you've made the necessary preparations in advance. Jesus' parable is about a wedding feast, but he goes even further by saying that if the master comes home to find his servants so well prepared, even in the middle of the night, he'll be willing to wait at table for them! Our friends would find it very strange if they arrived in response to our invitation only to find that no food had been prepared. Jesus expects us to be prepared for his return with a 'banquet' of obedience to him, and care for others.

3) One of the volunteers now brings out the vase of flowers, saying that it will help make the place more welcoming. It's not something you have to do, but an extra touch that makes guests feel more welcomed and cared for. Jesus wants us to be ready, not by grudgingly doing what he says but by welcoming him gladly into our lives.

4) Finally, get the volunteers to sit down and 'nod off' for a moment. As soon as their eyes are shut two more volunteers arrive unannounced as the guests. Oh dear! God doesn't want us to make domestic preparations, but when he arrives he wants to see us active in his service, by caring for those in need rather than indulging our material desires, and sharing his love with others. That's the way to be truly ready for him, and to hear him say, 'Well done'.

PROPER 15

Sunday between 14th and 20th August inclusive

As we continue through the middle of the holiday season, Matthew's Gospel reading in Year A tells of the faith of the Canaanite woman. In Year B the readings from chapter 6 of John's Gospel continue with Jesus explaining how that those who eat of his flesh and drink of his blood will have eternal life – a suitable outline address for this can be found in Book 1 of *Come to the Feast* under Maundy Thursday, the day when we give thanks for the institution of the Lord's Supper. The Year C Gospel from Luke 12 is also quite daunting in the context of all-age worship, and the focus here is on 'interpreting the times'.

Hymns

TRADITIONAL

- *Author of life divine*
- *Awake, awake: fling off the night*
- *Come, thou long-expected Jesus*
- *O thou, who at thy Eucharist didst pray*
- *Thine arm, O Lord, in days of old*

MODERN

- *Broken for me, broken for you*
- *Brother, sister, let me serve you*
- *Lord, we come to ask your healing*
- *O Lord, all the world belongs to you*
- *We believe in God the Father*

Readings

Year A Genesis 45:1-15 or Isaiah 56:1, 6-8; Romans 11:1-2a, 29-32; Matthew 15:(10-20) 21-28

Year B 1 Kings 2:10-12; 3:3-14 or Proverbs 9:1-6; Ephesians 5:15-20; John 6:51-58

Year C Isaiah 5:1-7 or Jeremiah 23:23-29; Hebrews 11:29-12:2; Luke 12:49-56

Confession

Lord God, full of mercy and compassion,
we confess to you our sin and failure.
Our mouths have not always
proclaimed your praise;
our feet have not always been swift
to follow where you lead;
our hearts are often unprepared
for you to come and dwell.
We are truly sorry and ask you to forgive us.
Make us clean we pray,
and by your Spirit strengthen us
to live in the way which pleases you,
to the glory of your name. Amen.

Absolution

God our Father,
who welcomes all who turn to him
in penitence and faith,
have mercy on you,
pardon and deliver you from all wrongdoing,
and lead you out from darkness
into the light of his eternal glory. Amen.

Prayer

Remembering that all our heavenly Father does
is faithful and just,
we bring him our requests and cares,
confident that he will keep his promise
to hear and answer us.
Lord, you are gracious and compassionate;
you remember your promise for ever.

Hear us as we pray for the Christian Church,
spread across the world yet one in your love:
for bishops, clergy and all Christian leaders;
for teachers and pastors;
for missionaries and evangelists;
for local congregations in every place.
We remember especially . . .
May all your people overcome divisions
of culture and pride,
and work together for your kingdom.
Lord, you are gracious and compassionate;
you remember your promise for ever.

Hear us as we pray for the world we live in,
damaged by human greed

yet still reflecting your love:
for politicians and diplomats
working in international relations;
for journalists and broadcasters
conveying information and opinion;
for financiers and economists
handling vast sums of money.
May those with great responsibility
use it wisely and for the good of all people.
Lord, you are gracious and compassionate;
you remember your promise for ever.

Hear us as we pray for the suffering and needy,
bearing their burden yet forgotten by society:
for the homeless and destitute;
for the exploited and downtrodden;
for the fearful and lonely;
for those we know and care for, especially . . .
May they know your arms of love
surrounding them,
your hand stretched out to reach them,
and your voice reassuring them
as you guide them through their troubles.
Lord, you are gracious and compassionate;
you remember your promise for ever.

Hear us as we commit ourselves to your care
and trust you for all that lies ahead.
May we rejoice in your presence
and go forward in your strength
until we reach the prize of your calling
in Christ Jesus.
Lord, you are gracious and compassionate;
**you remember your promise of mercy
in Jesus our Saviour
now and for evermore. Amen.**

All-age address 1

The account of Jesus healing a Canaanite (or Syro-Phoenician) woman's daughter will be familiar to many regular worshippers from the Prayer of Humble Access. In asking Jesus to heal her daughter, she knew she was acting out of turn, at least from the Jews' point of view, but she was willing to believe that this might not be a problem for Jesus. Even though he tested her faith initially, it was strong enough to stand firm, and Jesus willingly healed the child. The Jews believed strongly that God favoured them above the Gentiles, so

the true significance of this miracle wasn't lost on the writers of Matthew and Mark. Some preparation is needed in the form of four large cardboard boxes (ideally of the size used by removal firms for packing), one long side of each being covered with plain white paper. One word is written on each of these: 'race', 'class', 'gender', 'culture'. Fold the bottom and top flaps inside, and start with a forewarned volunteer who stands still while the boxes are lowered over his head, each one resting on the previous one. These are the barriers which people erect between each other, and which the healing power of Jesus destroys.

1) 'Race' should be on the top box. The woman from Syrian Phoenicia was of Greek origin according to Mark, and for Jews she was racially inferior as a Gentile. Racial bigotry is particularly hard to overcome as it relates to all kinds of deep-seated fears and assumptions about something no one has any control over. The woman herself recognised how she would be perceived by the Jews, but Jesus shows that the insulting term 'dogs' is not how he sees those of other races. At this point take away the box to reveal a bit more of the volunteer. Jesus treated people as equal, regardless of their racial background – we should do likewise.

2) Next should come the 'gender' box. We're fortunate to live at a time when women are accepted on the same level as men more than ever before – it's hard for us to imagine how difficult life was for a woman in Jesus' time. This woman had to overcome all the typical male prejudices of the day in order to claim Jesus' attention, and even the disciples were rather patronising. Maybe Jesus teased her gently (her reply possibly suggests she realised that), but she wasn't going to give up just because she was female. Now remove the second box, emphasising that women are just as valuable in God's sight as men.

3) 'Class' comes next, and while we may feel we do reasonably well on 'race' and 'gender' issues, the British have a strong class system which is hard to budge because it's so ingrained. This woman clearly recognised that her race and sex left

her at a disadvantage in Jewish society, or put her in 'a lower class'. Many factors affect how we view class – education, accent, family background, financial status – but none of them mattered to Jesus. Unlike us he never pigeon-holed people, but accepted everyone on their own merits. Indeed, he was far more accepting of people like this woman than of the self-righteous religious hypocrites who flaunted their social status. As you say this, remove the box, leaving just one.

4) The fourth box is marked 'culture', and perhaps contains a mixture of elements – race, religious belief, artistic expression . . . However, it's sometimes a barrier and we use it to stereotype people who see things a bit differently to ourselves. Jesus does the opposite, taking each person for who they are.

In performing this miracle Jesus is challenging all kinds of contemporary conventions, but he commends the woman's faith in a way which we see on only one other occasion in the Gospels (the Centurion whose servant was healed). She may be different in some ways but her faith puts most of Israel to shame. As you remove the last box, conclude by saying that God doesn't put people in boxes and build barriers around them. As Christians the love of Christ within us should help to break all of these down wherever we encounter them.

All-age address 2

Jesus' words in the passage from Luke have been much misunderstood and misrepresented – he's clearly describing the consequences of his mission, not its purpose. Since he never advocated conflict or violence, and clearly commended the peacemakers, Jesus can't be encouraging his followers to turn on their own families. But it's quite possible that within his own family there were potentially destructive tensions over his ministry, and this was certainly true for many of his followers. Therefore he wants them to interpret the 'signs of the times'. Since they could do it in simple matters such as forecasting the weather, surely they're also capable of interpreting correctly the events of his ministry. This outline aims to help show how God can be seen at work in the world and in our lives by looking at the way we draw conclusions from everyday events.

1) There are few areas of life which are subjected to media speculation and interpretation more than sport. Football tends to be the most widely acknowledged sport in most areas, though if cricket, rugby, motor racing or something else makes more sense in your community then use that. Whichever sport you take, pundits will be assessing the chances and merits of both teams and individuals, and the possible results of league and cup competitions. You may well find your local club is willing to let you have a team photo or something similar to use as a visual aid. It's hardly an exact science though. Past and present form may be a guide, key players may be injured, and weather conditions may be a factor, but there'll always be some guesswork. That's not true of God. He doesn't leave us guessing about what might happen next but guides us forward day by day as we trust him to lead us in the right paths.

2) At the same time the British also love speculating about the weather! It's a basic conversation starter, and we spend a great deal of time either commenting on present conditions or anticipating those to come. Either photocopy an outline map of the country and mark it with words such as 'windy', 'sunny and warm', 'rainy' or 'icy', or display a wall map, indicating what sort of weather each area will enjoy. Nowadays we can be very accurate in forecasting the weather, thanks to satellites and scientific advances. Jesus' contemporaries didn't have that advantage, though they were able to make reasonable attempts at predicting the weather. Sadly they didn't apply the same principles to God, and refused to recognise that he had sent his Son to be the promised Messiah. We don't know everything about God just because we're Christians, but we can be sure that he'll keep his promises and guide us in the right paths.

3) Finally bring out an item of little value (for example, an old cup and saucer, or an

ornament) and ask for opinions as to whether its value will increase with time – some answers will be more serious than others! While we know that certain things have become more valuable over a number of years, human estimations of their worth will fluctuate unpredictably. The religious leaders of Jesus' day seemed concerned only with fickle and temporary human values and were quite incapable of seeing in him things that related to eternity. The only values we can be sure of are the ones which last for ever, which is why Jesus tells us to make sure our treasure is stored up in heaven.

PROPER 16

Sunday between 21st and 27th August inclusive

As we read on through Matthew's Gospel in Year A we reach Peter's confession of Christ at Caesarea Philippi, while Year B sees the conclusion of the brief excursion into John 6. Year C brings us Luke's retelling of the healing of a crippled woman on the Sabbath, and the inevitable clash with the Jewish authorities.

Hymns

TRADITIONAL

- *Be thou my vision*
- *Bread of the world in mercy broken*
- *Eternal Ruler of the ceaseless round*
- *I'm not ashamed to own my Lord*
- *Lord Christ, who on thy heart*

MODERN

- *Alleluia, alleluia, give thanks to the risen Lord*
- *Be still and know that I am God*
- *Bless the Lord, my soul*
- *Cry 'Freedom!'*
- *You are the King of Glory*

Readings

Year A   Exodus 1:8-2:10 or Isaiah 51:1-6;
Romans 12:1-8; Matthew 16:13-20
Year B   1 Kings 8:(1, 6, 10-11) 22-30, 41-43 or
Joshua 24:1-2a, 14-18;
Ephesians 6:10-20; John 6:56-69
Year C   Jeremiah 1:4-10 or Isaiah 58:9b-14;
Hebrews 12:18-29; Luke 13:10-17

Confession

Merciful God, our loving Father,
we acknowledge before you with penitent hearts
our sins and shortcomings.
We have not always offered ourselves to you
as living sacrifices;
our lives are not always transformed
by a renewed mind;
we have not always used the gifts of the Spirit
to serve one another,
and build up the Body of Christ.
We ask you to pardon and forgive us
through your Son Jesus Christ,
so that we may not be conformed
to this world's pattern,
but instead discern your holy will
and live to your praise and glory. Amen.

Absolution

God our Father,
from whom comes every good and perfect gift,
grant you pardon for all
that has not been worthy of him,
forgive all your wrongdoing
and deliver you from all sin,
renewing you in mind
and transforming you into his likeness
for the sake of his Son,
Jesus Christ our Lord. Amen.

Prayer

Bringing the burden of our prayers to God,
who satisfies and renews us, we say,
Lord, you work justice for the oppressed;
make your ways known to all people.

We think of those oppressed
by the circumstances of their lives:
the street children in the world's great cities;
the inhabitants of refugee camps;
casualties of civil war or harsh government;
victims of crime and abuse.
Reassure and comfort them in their misery,
we pray,
and open the hearts of those who have wealth
to be generous and compassionate.
Lord, you work justice for the oppressed;
make your ways known to all people.

We think of those oppressed
by the consequences of their own behaviour:
drug addicts, alcoholics,
prisoners and young offenders.
Meet them at their point of deepest need,
we pray,
and heal them of all harmful influences
or past hurt.
Lord, you work justice for the oppressed;
make your ways known to all people.

We think of those oppressed
by illness or handicap:
those in hospital, the chronically sick,
the housebound, the frail and infirm elderly,
the depressed or mentally disturbed,
especially . . .
May they know your peace
and encouragement in their suffering,
and your healing love at work in their lives.
Lord, you work justice for the oppressed;
make your ways known to all people.

We think of the Church of which we are part,
called by you to proclaim
your message of release from captivity.
Open our eyes to recognise those
who are enslaved,
our lips to announce the good news
of freedom through Jesus Christ,
and our hearts and hands
to respond and act with your compassion.
Lord, you work justice for the oppressed;
make your ways known to all people,
so that the whole earth may sing your praise
and rejoice in your love,
through our Saviour Jesus Christ. Amen.

All-age address 1

The passage from Matthew 16 in which Peter confesses Jesus to be the promised Messiah can be well served by the address outline for the Sunday Next Before Lent, based on the Transfiguration. However, the vital point here is not just Peter's recognition of Jesus, but his acknowledgement of who he is and his response. For this you need to add a simple extra point about how we might react to someone well-known or important if we met them. For example you could ask for, or make, suggestions about the right way to respond to a request from the headteacher, the managing director, the prime minister or the Archbishop of Canterbury. You may need to ignore disrespectful answers, but in general terms if one of those asked us to do something, we'd be very likely to comply with the request! Conclude by saying that just as Peter fulfilled his commission from his Master, so, as we respond in faith to Christ and his calling, he will give us the strength to carry it out.

All-age address 2

The cost of following Jesus isn't the most popular subject for any sermon, but in an age of glossy, high-powered marketing and sales techniques it's an essential aspect of the Gospel to proclaim. In marketing or recruitment terms Jesus' refusal to shirk the realities of the Gospel would be fairly disastrous! However, it's both untrue to the Gospel and very misleading to imply that a decision to follow Christ will provide an escape route from all known problems and lead to a trouble free life. The following simple outline aims to present both the reality and the joys of the life of faith. It uses five simple cartoon-style drawings either on an OHP acetate or a flip-chart.

1) The first picture is of a steep mountain, with two small climber figures looking up and pointing to it. Start by saying that anyone wanting to reach the summit will need to think carefully about how tough it'll be to get there. There's no point tackling it if they haven't thought about the challenge it presents, and how they'll meet it.

2) The second picture is of our two climbers preparing their mountaineering gear – boots, rope and a pickaxe, for example. They obviously realise it's more than a stroll in the country! Jesus never promised that the Christian life would be as simple and undemanding as a gentle ramble – on the contrary, he was quite clear that at times it would be as tough as mountain-climbing. However, he did promise that his Holy Spirit would give us all the strength and equipment needed to meet the demands of following him.

3) The third picture is of the two climbers on a steep slope with their rucksacks on their backs – some indication of exertion and fatigue would add to the impact. Mountaineers have to carry their own equipment, and it sometimes feels very heavy! Jesus said that 'carrying our cross' is an essential part of the life of faith, and there'll be times when we feel like giving it up or trying another way. Perseverance is a vital aspect of discipleship.

4) The fourth picture is of one climber lying down, holding his leg in pain, while the other one is helping him. On our Christian journey there'll also be times when we fall or get hurt. Jesus has promised that he will be there alongside us, to heal, to pick us up and dust us down, and set us on our way again.

5) The final picture is of the two climbers on top of the mountain, with a flag flying and big smiles on their faces. After all the exertion and bruises they've made it, and they're enjoying the wonderful view and the fact that they're on the summit! The enjoyment is greater because they've struggled to get there. The Christian life isn't easy, but if we keep going in God's strength we know that one day we'll have the joy of seeing him ourselves and being with him for ever.

All-age address 3

Luke's account of Jesus healing a crippled woman on the Sabbath is focused primarily on the subsequent dispute with the authorities. Having lots of detailed rules suited them well as it kept them in control, but where those rules worked against the welfare of those in need, or against the true worship of God, Jesus was more than willing to disregard them. The outline address for Proper 3 is equally applicable to this passage. However, you'll need to include a few words of explanation about the Sabbath rules, and why the leader of the synagogue was cross with both Jesus and those who'd come for healing. More important still, emphasise that Jesus' priority was to make the woman whole, breaking the power of evil over her and bringing glory to God – what better thing to do on the Sabbath! As Christians, our primary rule must be the 'law of love', and all other laws must keep in line with that, however important they are.

Proper 17

Sunday between 28th August and 3rd September inclusive

In Year A this week Matthew recalls Jesus teaching the disciples that he must die, and telling them about the cost of following him – suitable outline addresses for this can be found either in Proper 7 (address 1) or Proper 16 (address 1). In Year B we return to Mark in chapter 7, and hear Jesus teaching the people about what's clean and unclean in God's sight. Luke, in Year C, quotes Jesus' teaching on status and service.

Hymns

TRADITIONAL

- *All my hope on God is founded*
- *Be still, my soul*
- *Father of heaven, whose love profound*
- *Take up thy cross, the Saviour said*
- *The head that once was crowned with thorns*

MODERN

- *Be still, for the presence of the Lord*
- *From heaven you came*
- *God forgave my sin*
- *Moses, I know you're the man*
- *One more step along the world I go*

Readings

Year A   Exodus 3:1-15 or Jeremiah 15:15-21;
Romans 12:9-21; Matthew 16:21-28
Year B   Song of Solomon 2:8-13 or
Deuteronomy 4:1-2, 6-9; James 1:17-27;
Mark 7:1-8, 14-15, 21-23
Year C   Jeremiah 2:4-13 or Proverbs 25:6-7 or
Ecclesiasticus 10:12-18;
Hebrews 13:1-8, 15-16; Luke 14:1, 7-14

Confession

Hear us, O God of our salvation,
as we cry to you for forgiveness and help.
We have sinned against you and our neighbour
by pursuing status for ourselves
instead of the welfare of others;
by cultivating public image
instead of private devotion;
by following the wide road of comfort and ease
instead of the rugged path that takes us to you.
Have mercy on us, we pray,
cleanse us from all that defiles,
and by your Spirit set our feet
in the way of peace that leads to eternal life,
through our Lord Jesus Christ. Amen.

Absolution

God, who saves and heals all
who repent and turn from evil,
have mercy on you,
forgive all your sins,
make your hearts clean
from every kind of wrong,
and strengthen you to obey his will,
not seeking reward or honour
but the growth of his kingdom,
through Jesus Christ our Lord. Amen.

Intercession

We turn to our Father God,
from whom comes every good and perfect gift,
bringing our thanksgiving and prayers
and saying,
Lord, as we hear your word,
help us to do what it says.

Your word tells us not to discriminate
or show favouritism.
We pray for those who feel marginalised
or exploited by the powerful and wealthy –
victims of injustice and greed,
the downtrodden and ignored,
left on the edges of society
without resources or hope.
Help us to stand alongside them,
showing mercy and sharing your love.
Lord, as we hear your word,
help us to do what it says.

Your word tells us that our faith
must be accompanied by action.
We pray for those who go out
in the name of Christ
to bring aid and relief,

to set captives free,
to reach out to the poor and unwanted,
and especially we pray . . .
Help us to show that our faith is alive and real
through acts of practical care and generosity.
Lord, as we hear your word,
help us to do what it says.

Your word tells us that true faith
involves caring for the suffering and defenceless.
We pray for those in distress
as a result of illness, bereavement,
anxiety or personal crisis,
especially . . .
Help us to befriend the friendless,
support the weak, and comfort the hurting.
Lord, as we hear your word,
help us to do what it says.

Your word tells us that we are justified
by our faith and actions together.
We pray for our own church fellowship
as part of the worldwide Body of Christ,
that our words and behaviour may show
the reality of what we believe.
Help us to speak words
of encouragement and kindness,
rather than criticising and condemning;
to share the mind of Christ,
and count the needs and interests of others
above our own;
to treat others without fear or favour,
recognising that all are equal in your sight.
Lord, as we hear your word,
help us to do what it says,
that we may be built up in our faith
and strengthened in doing your will,
through Jesus Christ our Lord. Amen.

All-age address 1

So many of the conflicts which arose between
Jesus and the religious leaders were to do with
keeping rules. The argument over clean and
unclean foods was no exception, and, as usual,
Jesus' opponents had completely missed the
point. Eating certain foods doesn't make us
unclean, nor does abstaining from them mean
that we're clean! No doubt the teachers of the
law were ritually clean, and proud of it, but
they failed to understand that their attitudes
and intransigence made them unclean in God's

eyes. This outline aims to make that distinction,
and to do so requires careful preparation in
advance. You'll need a little washing powder,
detergent and a bar of soap, plus a piece of
fabric which is no longer needed (an old T-shirt,
for example), and a plate heavily stained by
food. A volunteer with grubby hands is your
final visual aid, and for each of these a bowl of
hot water is necessary (best brought in by
another volunteer at the appropriate time). If
you prefer not to get wet yourself, you'll need
another volunteer to do the washing.

1) Take the detergent and extol the virtues of
   its cleansing properties before producing
   the dirty plate. Having asked for opinions
   about whether the stains can be removed,
   place it in the first bowl of water and add
   some detergent. It may need to soak for a
   while but eventually a bit of scrubbing
   should make it usable again. This is surface
   dirt, which washes off quite easily. The
   Pharisees treated sin as a disobedience to
   their rules, which could be dealt with by
   keeping to the prescribed rituals, but this
   was a superficial and inadequate view.

2) Beforehand rub the T-shirt well in garden
   soil, so that it becomes a nasty shade of grey.
   Do a quick commercial for the soap-powder
   before holding up the soiled garment, and
   then dip it in the second bowl, adding a
   little soap powder and rubbing vigorously.
   It should be possible to make a visible
   difference fairly quickly. Point out that in
   this case the dirt is much more ingrained. Sin
   is deeply ingrained into our lives, making
   us unclean. Jesus came to deal not just
   with visible sins, but with the deeply held
   attitudes which often underlie them.

3) Now your unwashed volunteer comes
   forward, and you show the congregation
   his hands, eliciting noises of disgust. Offer
   the bar of soap and the third bowl, again
   expounding its qualities. This is also surface
   dirt, and should come off fairly easily. Explain
   that the Pharisees could only see the surface.
   Your volunteer's hands may be clean, but if
   he or she had a cold or virus, soap would
   be of no use whatever – to treat it internally
   they'd need antibiotics or Lemsip!

Conclude by saying that Jesus challenged the superficiality of his opponents – the real problem wasn't what could be seen (the food they ate) but what lay beneath the surface (wrong thoughts leading to wrong behaviour). God doesn't accept us because we keep to certain rituals. When we recognise and repent of our sins, he forgives us and cleans us up from within through the death of Jesus.

All-age address 2

Status has always been a major factor in any society. Pecking orders, recognition and symbols of status were as influential in Jesus' day as in ours. Having been invited to a meal with a prominent Pharisee, he observed how many of the guests sought an honoured place at the table – a major status symbol in that culture. On a practical level that could clearly lead to embarrassment or humiliation, but Jesus also contrasts this with status in God's kingdom. Each society inevitably has its own different social levels, based on a variety of factors, and all the attempts in this century to make everyone equal have come unstuck. The Christian faith goes far beyond imposing a new social structure (which will create its own new distinctions before long) and overturns our human aspirations. For this simple outline a few recognisable status symbols are all that's needed – pictures pasted on card or model replicas may be easier to obtain than the real thing!

1) First show a picture or small model of a Ferrari. A large, fast car is often a symbol of status based on power. The owner obviously has plenty of cash, but wants to demonstrate more than that. Somehow, you wouldn't feel like arguing with the owner of such a vehicle! Human beings are very tempted to exercise power over each other, but status in God's kingdom is based on humility.

2) Next show a picture of a Rolex watch. Here's a symbol of extreme 'good taste', the sign of pedigree and class. The owner of this is definitely keen on cultural superiority. Our human reaction is often to find a way of proving that we're in some way superior to others, and those on the wrong end of this will accuse us of 'snobbery'. It's a futile exercise, because no one can really define what 'good taste' is! Jesus tells his hearers not to spend their money on things to create an impression, but on providing for those who can't repay or give any return.

3) Now display a picture of a major social event, with elegantly dressed guests. Some people show off by being seen in the right company, to show they're socially 'upmarket'. God regards all people as equal, and while the various social layers may have a limited short-term function, they don't reflect God's view of humankind. Instead of promoting self-image, Jesus tells us to take a humbler position, as he himself did. He was humiliated on the cross, but now has the most honoured place in God's kingdom. Like him, we're to count the interests and welfare of others above our own, not looking for human acclaim but accepting that our reward will be from our heavenly Father.

PROPER 18

Sunday between 4th and 10th September inclusive

As schools and colleges start out on a new academic year, and many people return from holidays, we're working our way towards the end of the cycle of readings from each Gospel. In Year A Matthew relates Jesus' teaching on forgiveness, and in Year B we read Mark's account of the healing of the Syro-Phoenician woman's daughter, as well as the healing of a man who was both deaf and mute. In Year C Luke in his turn sets out Jesus' teaching on the cost of being a disciple. A suitable outline address for the passage from Mark can be found at Proper 15 (address 1), while for Luke either Proper 7 (address 1) or Proper 16 (address 1) can be used.

Hymns

TRADITIONAL

- *All things bright and beautiful*
- *Amazing grace*
- *New songs of celebration render*
- *Jesus calls us: oe'r the tumult*
- *There's a wideness in God's mercy*

MODERN

- *Lord, for the years*
- *Kyrie eleison*
- *Come and see*
- *From the sun's rising*
- *Lord, the light of your love*

Readings

Year A   Exodus 12:1-14 or Ezekiel 33:7-11;
         Romans 13:8-14; Matthew 18:15-20
Year B   Proverbs 22:1-2, 8-9, 22-23 or
         Isaiah 35:4-7a;
         James 2:1-10, (11-13), 14-17;
         Mark 7:24-37
Year C   Jeremiah 18:1-11 or
         Deuteronomy 30:15-20;
         Philemon 1-21; Luke 14:25-33

Confession

Lord God,
you have taught us that love
is the fulfilment of the law,
but we have not obeyed its demands.
We repent and seek your pardon;
Lord, forgive and renew us.

Your law demands
that we do not harm our neighbours
but love them as ourselves.
For the damage done,
through careless words and selfish actions,
we repent and seek your pardon;
Lord, forgive and renew us.

Your law demands that we do not covet or steal
anything belonging to our neighbours.
For paying more attention
to our own well-being
than to the needs and concerns of others,
we repent and seek your pardon;
Lord, forgive and renew us.

Your law demands that we put aside
the deeds of darkness
and walk in your light.
For trying to disguise our sins
and pretend we can hide them from you
or each other,
we repent and seek your pardon;
Lord, forgive and renew us.

Your law demands that we fulfil
the continuing debt to love one another.
For living only to ourselves,
and neglecting your command
to love one another and you
with a sincere and true heart,
we repent and seek your pardon;
Lord, forgive and renew us.
Give us grace to clothe ourselves
with the Lord Jesus Christ,
and live to his praise and glory,
in whose name we pray. Amen.

Absolution

God, whose laws are trustworthy and perfect,
have mercy on you,
forgive all your sins

and bring you to newness of life,
that you may no longer live to self
but to the glory of our Saviour Jesus Christ.
Amen.

Prayer

Our Father God,
whose hand is always upon us,
knows the deepest desires of our hearts,
even when we cannot find words
to contain them.
We reach out to him in faith
as we bring him our prayers,
spoken and unspoken, saying together,
Lord, you are more ready to answer
than we to ask;
hear us as we pray in faith.

We pray for the Church in every part
of the world
as it worships and serves you,
especially where your people
are called to withstand great pressure
if they remain faithful to you.
Bless and guide by your Spirit
all Christian leaders, teachers and pastors,
preachers and evangelists,
that through their ministry
your people may be built up in faith and love.
Especially we pray . . .
Lord, you are more ready to answer
than we to ask;
hear us as we pray in faith.

We pray for the world we are called to serve,
remembering the needs
which so often threaten to overwhelm,
and the victims of disaster,
injustice and inhumanity.
Bless and guide our own country
and the nations of the world,
that they may be willing to confront evil
and corruption,
and give them courage
to uphold the standards of your kingdom.
Especially we pray . . .
Lord, you are more ready to answer
than we to ask;
hear us as we pray in faith.

We pray for our families,
friends and loved ones,
naming before you those in particular need
as a result of illness, bereavement,
sadness or confusion, especially . . .
Give them the strength
to endure their present time of distress,
and the confidence to believe
that you will bring them through
into renewed joy and deepened faith.
Lord, you are more ready to answer
than we to ask;
hear us as we pray in faith.

We pray for our own faith and Christian witness
as we seek to bring your love to those around us.
Make us bold to proclaim your good news
and faithful in following you.
Lord, you are more ready to answer
than we to ask;
**hear us as we pray in faith,
and answer us according to your perfect will,
through Jesus Christ our Lord. Amen.**

All-age address

This address outline is based on today's passage from Matthew 18, not emphasising legal procedures but concentrating instead on positive and negative relationships. You'll need a sheet of A3 paper and a suitably sized frame from an art supplies shop (if you opt for a photograph frame, don't forget to remove the glass!). On the sheet of paper write words describing relationships – for example, 'family', 'friends', 'business partners', 'colleagues', 'acquaintances', 'fellow Christians'– and when it's full, fit it into the frame with sellotape or blutack. Next take some smaller pieces of paper and write on each of them a behaviour or attitude which harms relationships – 'jealousy', 'envy', 'conflict', 'rivalry', 'gossip', 'malice', 'hatred', 'resentment'. One of these will be wrapped in turn around a tennis ball, which will be thrown at the paper in the frame. Finally, take some similar pieces of paper and write on them words such as 'love', 'kindness', 'patience', 'forgiveness', 'generosity', 'compassion' and 'sensitivity'.

1) Take the first piece of paper and wrap it

around the ball, and explain that in the frame are words which describe relationships. Ask a child to throw the paper-covered ball at the sheet in the frame, which should tear easily. After this has happened retrieve the ball and ask the child what's written on it. If the word is 'jealousy', explain how jealousy can destroy family life. Repeat this process about six times, on each occasion explaining how relationships are destroyed by such attitudes and behaviour.

2) When the paper is way beyond repair, ask the congregation what sort of things would restore relationships again. You should get some helpful suggestions, and when this is done, use the second set of smaller pieces of paper with the 'positive' words to repair the large sheet, pointing out that these things will build up our relationships with one another.

Conclude by referring to Jesus' words. He knew that even when things go a bit wrong, honesty and integrity count for a great deal. Only as a last resort, if the other person continues the disagreement, are we to break off the relationship. But more important than disagreeing is agreeing before God, because God made us to live in relationship. Where we do that harmoniously and constructively he promises to be present, and to answer prayers, because prayer that comes from such an environment won't be selfish, but in line with his will.

PROPER 19

Sunday between 11th and 17th September inclusive

This Sunday's Year A Gospel reading from Matthew is Jesus' parable of the unforgiving servant. Year B consists of Mark's account of Peter's confession of Christ at Caesarea Philippi, for which a suitable outline address can be found under Proper 16 (All-age address 1). Year C contains two of Luke's three very famous parables about being lost and found.

Hymns

TRADITIONAL

- *Forgive our sins as we forgive*
- *Hark, my soul, it is the Lord*
- *I will sing the wondrous story*
- *Lord Jesus, think on me*
- *My God, how wonderful thou art*

MODERN

- *All heaven declares*
- *All that I am, all that I do*
- *I love you, Lord*
- *Jesus, Jesus, holy and anointed one*
- *My Lord, what love is this*

Readings

Year A   Exodus 14:19-31 or Genesis 50:15-21;
Romans 14:1-12; Matthew 18:21-35
Year B   Proverbs 1:20-33 or Isaiah 50:4-9a;
James 3:1-12; Mark 8:27-38
Year C   Jeremiah 4:11-12, 22-28 or
Exodus 32:7-14; 1 Timothy 1:12-17;
Luke 15:1-10

Confession

Gracious Father, whose love never ceases,
whose mercy never fails,
we confess with penitent hearts
the sins we have committed against you
and each other.
We find trivial faults in others
while ignoring our own wrongdoing;
we are critical and ungenerous
in our judgements
while overlooking our own failings;
we seek your pardon
without forgiving those who have wronged us.
Forgive us and be merciful to us, we pray,
and, in receiving your forgiveness,
make us willing to forgive others,
through Christ our Lord. Amen.

Absolution

God, who is the source of forgiveness and grace,
deliver you from all your sins,
and in his mercy restore you to his service,
that you may be freed from the chains of guilt
into the joy of eternal life
in Jesus Christ our Lord. Amen.

Prayer

Our Father in heaven knows
the thoughts of our hearts,
even when we find it difficult to express them.
We bring him our requests and concerns saying,
Lord, hear us as we pray to you,
and accept the prayer of our hearts.

We ask you to bless and guide your Church
as it proclaims the good news;
give wisdom to all who speak in your name:
preachers, evangelists, and leaders,
lay or ordained.
May their words be wise and sensitive,
rooted in the truth, framed by your love,
directed to the building up of your people
in unity and the establishment of your kingdom.
Lord, hear us as we pray to you,
and accept the prayer of our hearts.

We ask you to bless all who use words
to direct the course of this world's affairs:
politicians and lawyers,
journalists and broadcasters,
academics and executives.
May their words be honest and positive,
founded on integrity,
fuelled by concern for the poor and vulnerable,
promoting justice and peace.
Lord, hear us as we pray to you,
and accept the prayer of our hearts.

We ask you to bless all who use words
to nurture and encourage:
healthcare and social workers,
carers, counsellors and teachers.
May their words be kind and supportive,
based on compassion and commitment,
filled with hope and courage.
Lord, hear us as we pray to you,
and accept the prayer of our hearts.

We ask you to bless those who find it impossible
to express their pain and suffering in words:
the physically or mentally sick,
the bereaved and lonely,
the distressed and despairing,
especially . . .
May they know you alongside
them in the dark times,
understanding their deepest longings
and holding them in your loving arms.
Lord, hear us as we pray to you,
and accept the prayer of our hearts.

We ask for your blessing on all we do and say,
that our minds may be directed by your love
and our tongues brought under your control,
so that in word and action
our lives may bring glory to your name.
Lord, hear us as we pray to you,
and accept the prayer of our hearts
for the sake of your Son,
Jesus Christ our Lord. Amen.

All-age address 1

Few concepts are more difficult to convey in simple terms than forgiveness. In large measure we understand it through experiencing it, and in any normal cross-section of people there will be a wide range of experiences of being forgiven. Jesus wasn't unfamiliar with this, as his parable of the unforgiving servant bears out. Here he challenges a contemporary understanding of forgiveness, in which, as Peter rather naively indicates, it had become a cog in the legal machine. Jesus puts the emphasis instead on the love and mercy which alone can bring it about. Twentieth-century society is equally judgemental and unforgiving towards those who are unable or unwilling to conform, so Jesus' teaching is just as relevant today. This outline focuses on three aspects of forgiveness brought out by Jesus – it's based entirely on mercy, it depends on us recognising our need of it, and we can only receive it to the extent that we're prepared to give it to others. It needs three well-briefed volunteers and the necessary props.

1) Two volunteers are each engaged in painting a picture on adjacent tables. One bumps into the other's table fairly violently, thus spoiling their work of art and knocking over the water pot. The other jumps up and threatens to do the same in return. At this point step in and ask whether that response is deserved or constructive. It's unlikely that many will answer 'yes' to either question. Explain that our natural 'sense of justice' wants to see the guilty party experience the suffering caused to others, but we know that won't achieve anything or improve the situation. The only way forward is for the second person to forgive the first for their clumsiness and to set the record straight, so that the matter is forgotten and their relationship resumed. In Jesus' parable the only solution was for the king to forgive the servant who owed him so much and set him free.

2) This time the second volunteer deliberately smears the first's picture, causing great indignation and a similar threat of reprisal. Before this is taken further, intervene, asking what the appropriate responses to this situation might be. 'Forgiveness' and 'contrition' (or words expressing the same idea) are the ideas to bring out. Smearing the culprit's own picture would do no more than make the victim feel better (or 'avenged'), so forgiveness has to be the answer, however undeserved it may seem. However, the guilty one also needs to acknowledge that wrong has been done, which can only be rectified by receiving freely offered forgiveness. Jesus wants us to understand that our heavenly Father is like this, willing to forgive the worst things we've ever done provided that we accept our wrongdoing, receive his forgiveness and live as his followers.

3) The final scene involves the third volunteer, also painting at a table adjacent to the other two. The second volunteer again spoils the first's artwork, and after threatened retribution receives forgiveness. While this is happening, the third accidentally makes a slight mark on the second's painting. On discovering this, the former culprit, now the victim, threatens to ruin the third's work. Despite many entreaties, and damage barely visible, the second carries on and destroys the third's picture, at which point the first loses his rag and destroys the second's. This is the sort of situation Jesus was describing; it demonstrates his point that forgiveness, which by definition must be given rather than earned, cannot be received if it isn't given. We demonstrate our own experience of God's forgiveness by forgiving those who harm or upset us, not out of duty but from our heart.

All-age address 2

Luke gathers together three of Jesus' best-known parables about things which are lost – a sheep, a coin and a son. Since most of us lose things, in some cases fairly regularly, we can identify readily with his points. This outline follows a similar pattern to Luke 15, and needs a few visual aids – a small family pet, such as a hamster or one of the smaller breeds of dog (if practicable!), a 'lost pet' notice, a set of keys (optional), a small piece of jewellery (not valuable!) and a fictitious 'missing person' poster.

1) Start by saying that everyone loses things from time to time – maybe an umbrella, the pen by the telephone, or a letter. Mostly these aren't too important or valuable, and they often turn up later in some unexpected place. Occasionally, something more precious or vital goes astray, and then we send out a full-scale search party and don't stop looking until it's been found. If time allows say that you've lost your keys and can't get back into your home until you've found them. 'Hide' them somewhere to be discovered and quickly returned. Now produce the pet and the notice offering a reward for finding a lost one, and indicate that the shepherd had a similar relationship with his sheep as we might with our pets. He was willing to go to any lengths to find one that was lost. God was also prepared to do anything to bring us back to himself, too, whatever the cost to him. And he's as happy to receive us back as we would be to find our lost pet alive and well.

2) Now produce the ring (ideally one that looks like an engagement ring), and ask a married or engaged woman how she would feel if she lost her ring – this will only elicit one answer! The woman in Jesus' parable would have had similar emotions about losing her coin, which was probably part of her dowry. We don't know its exact value, but what mattered to her was its association. So she turned the whole house upside down until she found it. Again, there was great joy when she did so. The picture of God's saving activity is the same, but significantly a woman is used here as the example – a radical idea for its day!

3) Finally, hold up the missing person poster, pointing out as you do so that the person isn't lost like a toddler in a supermarket – this person knows his whereabouts but his family and friends don't. He's lost to them. There are many anguished families who wonder about one of their relatives who hasn't been heard of for ages. The father in Jesus' parable had no idea where his son was, or whether he'd ever see him again, but he never gave up hope, and was always on the lookout. When the son finally decided to return, he was still some way from home when his father rushed to greet him and gave him a royal welcome. The son didn't deserve this welcome (as his elder brother soon pointed out) but the past was forgiven and the joy overwhelming. Jesus is making the same point again, but much more poignantly.

Finish by saying that we are God's children, and it hurts him when we go away from him; there's nothing he won't do to bring us back and restore us to where we once were, however bad or daft our actions. His joy is as unlimited as his forgiveness.

PROPER 20

Sunday between 18th and 24th September inclusive

As we approach the end of this long stretch of 'Ordinary Time' we reach Matthew 20 in Year A, and Jesus' parable of the workers in the vineyard. Year B's passage from Mark 9 starts with Jesus' prediction of his death and resurrection to his bemused disciples, followed by their arguments about status. In Year C, Luke recounts the parable of the shrewd manager.

Hymns

TRADITIONAL

- *All people that on earth do dwell*
- *Father, Lord of all Creation*
- *Glorious things of thee are spoken*
- *Help us to help each other, Lord*
- *I come with joy*

MODERN

- *For I'm building a people of power*
- *He's got the whole world in his hand*
- *Let there be love shared among us*
- *Love is his word*
- *Peace is flowing like a river*

Readings

Year A   Exodus 16:2-15 or Jonah 3:10-4:11;
         Philippians 1:21-30; Matthew 20:1-16
Year B   Proverbs 31:10-31 or Wisdom 1:16-2:1,
         12-22 or Jeremiah 11:18-20;
         James 3:13-4:3, 7-8a; Mark 9:30-37
Year C   Jeremiah 8:18-9:1 or Amos 8:4-7;
         1 Timothy 2:1-7; Luke 16:1-13

Confession

God of grace and glory,
we confess with sorrow
that we have failed to live up to your calling.
We repent of our waywardness
and straying from your path;
our carelessness and lack of concern for others;
our self-will and rejection of your ways.

Forgive all our sin, we pray,
and renew us by your Spirit,
that our hearts may be ruled
by the peace of Christ,
and our lives dedicated to
his glory. Amen.

Absolution

God our Father,
who calls us to follow and serve him,
pardon all your sin,
forgive all your failures,
and restore you to the joy
of being one with him and each other,
through Jesus Christ our Lord. Amen.

Prayer

As those called by God our Father
to work for his kingdom,
we bring to him our prayers and requests
for the Church and the world, saying,
Master, receive these prayers,
and strengthen us to work for you.

We bring our prayers
for the work of your Church
in every part of the world,
where there is poverty and hardship,
where there is crime and violence,
where there is despair and fear,
especially . . .
May all Christian people strive together
for the good of the whole world
and bring closer your reign of justice and peace.
Master, receive these prayers,
and strengthen us to work for you.

We bring our prayers
for the work of reconciliation
and relief of suffering
which continues across the world
despite the forces of evil and destruction,
especially in . . .
May all aid workers and carers
be strengthened and encouraged by your Spirit
as they counter hostility
and suspicion with your love.
Master, receive these prayers,
and strengthen us to work for you.

We bring our prayers
for the work of government and leadership
in our own country and throughout the world,
especially . . .
May all politicians, community leaders and
decision-makers
acknowledge your ultimate authority
acting wisely and rightly in the interests of all.
Master, receive these prayers,
and strengthen us to work for you.

We bring our prayers
for our families and friends,
those who matter most to us
and whose concerns touch our hearts.
We remember too those who suffer
as a result of illness, infirmity, anxiety or grief,
especially . . .
May they know your healing touch on their lives
and the peace of your abiding presence.
Master, receive these prayers,
and strengthen us to work for you.

We bring to you ourselves, our work and rest,
our thinking and speaking,
and ask that your Holy Spirit will guide us
into your ways and truth.
May your love and joy be seen in all we do.
Master, receive these prayers,
and strengthen us to work for you,
seeking no reward
apart from knowing we do your will,
for the sake of Christ our Lord. Amen.

All-age address 1

Taken at face value, the parable of the workers in the vineyard wouldn't endear itself to trade union leaders seeking equal treatment and opportunity for all employees. In fact, Jesus based this parable on what was then considered normal practice, but his message clearly isn't about fair employment practices. What he wants his hearers to understand is the way in which the values of the kingdom turn our human ideas on their heads. The landowner here is scrupulously fair and abides by the agreement he's made with each worker, but, more than that, goes out himself to find and hire them (not something a landowner would normally do). The biggest surprise, however,

is his generosity to those he employed last, and his refusal to differentiate between his workers. Unlike us, God doesn't operate on the basis of merit and reward, but on grace and kindness, even to those we might regard as undeserving (an unmistakable message for the legalistic Pharisees).

This outline picks up the theme of surprising generosity, and, while simple, it does require a bit of preparatory shopping! You'll need an expensive-looking box of chocolates, a large bar of chocolate, a Mars Bar (or equivalent) and enough small wrapped sweets to give out to most of the congregation. You might also want to prime one or two people in advance.

1) Start by saying how important it is to express thanks to people, and explain that you want to say 'thank you' to certain people who work very hard for your church. Then take a selection of the small wrapped sweets in a dish and ask a long-serving member of the congregation to choose one as a thank-you for all his hard work. Repeat this several times with, for example, a musician or choir member, a churchwarden or senior lay leader, a sidesman or steward, a PCC member, a flower-arranger or a member of the cleaning rota. Finish by stressing that you wanted to be absolutely fair to everyone.

2) Now move on to point out that we often see things differently. To someone who's done a bit more than they needed to, you might give a Mars Bar; to someone who takes a fair amount of responsibility, you might present a large bar of chocolate; and for someone who's really important or hard-working, you might go mad and buy a special box of chocolates. With each point produce the relevant item! There's nothing wrong with this kind of generosity, but it works entirely on the basis of rewarding people according to what they've done.

3) God is completely different, and Jesus' parable shows how, like the landowner, he treats everyone with the same degree of generosity. The workers he took on near the end of the day received exactly the same as those who'd worked all through the day. He wasn't being unfair to those who had

worked all day – they were receiving more than fair payment for a day's work, and their complaints were based on jealousy. The Pharisees and Scribes didn't like Jesus' concern for the poor and needy, and felt they should receive better treatment in comparison. But God deals with people on the basis of his love, not on whether they've fulfilled certain obligations. Conclude by explaining that you're going to give every-one a wrapped sweet, not as a reward for services rendered but as a picture of God's love, which is given freely to everyone, regardless of background or achievement.

All-age address 2

Status-seeking is all too familiar in our society, but while people may use different symbols these days to indicate their social position, they're not doing anything new. Fighting over a 'pecking order' occurs in almost any group, not least the Church, so it's not surprising that it cropped up among the disciples, even though they should have known better if they'd been listening to Jesus' teaching. But Jesus heard them squabbling, and they must have felt distinctly embarrassed to admit what they'd been arguing over. Jesus used a live 'visual aid' (a small child) to illustrate the attitude of those who are part of God's kingdom, and this outline follows suit, using the idea of the 'balloon debate'. You'll need four well-briefed volunteers who can play an impromptu part in a lively and relaxed way.

1) The first volunteer brings in a certificate of some educational achievement (real or fictitious!) and goes on about how important it is for our church to have people who are well-qualified, intelligent, capable of making right decisions, etc. After a moment or two, interrupt him and ask whether one or two other gifts might be useful in church, to which he responds that someone needs to make decisions if the church is to survive.

2) The second volunteer appears with a cheque book and set of accounts, and immediately launches into a speech on the importance of good accounting practice and wise stewardship. He adds a bit about rich Christians being able to put more money into the church, but you cut across his self-promotion by asking if one or two other talents might also help the church to move forwards.

3) The third volunteer brings in a sheet of music (and possibly a small instrument) and tells everyone how vital creative and artistic people are to the church, as without them there'd be no beautiful liturgy or music, no drama or artistic work, and so on. Before his head gets too big, break into his monologue with the same question – can the church get anywhere just with these talents?

4) Now the final volunteer appears, brandishing cleaning equipment, and starts to discourse on the problems the church would have if there weren't ordinary people who roll up their sleeves and get on with the real work. Before the 'too many chiefs and not enough Indians' argument sets in, the others interrupt and assert their own importance, and a hot debate is clearly brewing.

5) Interrupt by telling them off for arguing and showing off, and emphasise the importance of good leadership! Conclude at this point by emphasising that the church needs people who are good at thinking, at accounting, at music and at cleaning – they all play a vital part in its life and mission. The most important role of all, though, is that of the servant, who isn't concerned about status or who he's seen with, but instead gets on with serving his master. Jesus showed the disciples a small child, who would have been totally overlooked in their quarrel, and pointed out that in God's kingdom those who welcomed that child in effect welcomed him too. God cares for the least important in human society as much as he does the influential and significant, and those who follow his ways must do likewise.

All-age address 3

The parable of the shrewd manager is one of Jesus' more puzzling utterances, at least at face value, since he seems to be condoning dishonesty and lack of integrity. Few parables have been interpreted in so many different ways, and it isn't entirely obvious, even on closer inspection, exactly what point Jesus is making. The manager in question was probably incompetent rather than dishonest – he's wasted his master's resources rather than stolen them – but he's under no illusion that his job is on the line, so he sets out to make preparations for what life might be like after the books have been audited and he's facing unemployment. It's likely that some of Jesus' hearers were reformed tax-collectors who would have related to this story of a man protecting his own interests, but Jesus would hardly have been commending them to continue with dubious financial practices. The man's personal honesty isn't the central point here. This outline focuses on the issue raised by Jesus of preparing for a new life, and requires a few simple props related to moving house.

1) It's more than likely that someone in the congregation will have moved house in the recent past, and they may be willing to answer a few simple questions about the process. Why did you move? How did you choose where to move to? Were you sad to leave your old home? Did you do much hard work? Have you still got boxes to unpack? Did you settle in quickly in the new one? You could even use a couple of estate agent's leaflets to illustrate this. Explain that the man in Jesus' parable knew he'd have to move. He hadn't done his job well and knew he'd be given the sack. So he thought carefully and decided to make preparations for his new life.

2) Some people find they must move as a result of financial difficulties. This man thought about his financial situation (you could use a cheque book or financial document to illustrate this point). Moving house is expensive, but this man was also faced with losing his income, so he used his remaining work time to ease the economic burden of his employer's clients by reducing their debt repayments (God had forbidden the Jews to charge interest, though it's not clear whether the employer was doing so here). In effect he was buying their favour and friendship.

3) Sometimes people move to a smaller house because of health problems. This employee thought about his health situation, and recognised he was no longer strong enough to do hard physical work, the only alternative open to him apart from the humiliation of begging. He would need the help of others.

4) Sometimes people move to be nearer family or friends, and others know they'll be moving away from their present social circle. This man thought about his social situation and realised at once that he'd need friends in order to survive. His employer commended his shrewdness, if not his integrity, and Jesus uses him to warn his hearers that they too must recognise that their present circumstances will change, one day for ever. Healthy relationships are more important in eternal terms than a healthy bank balance. We must also recognise that we need each other's help in this life.

Conclude by adding that Jesus encourages us to be honest and act with integrity in matters both small and large, and warns us that we can't serve both material possessions and God. Like the Pharisees, we must learn that the values of God's kingdom are totally different from ours.

PROPER 21

Sunday between 25th September
and 1st October inclusive

At this time of year many churches will be celebrating Harvest Festival, so in Year C Luke's account of the parable of Dives and Lazarus has a particular significance in terms of using what God has given us in order to provide for the poor. In Year B, too, Mark reminds us that Jesus often taught people along these lines. In Year A the passage from Matthew starts off with the dispute over Jesus' authority, continuing with the parable of the two sons, which shows that actions matter more than words for those who follow Jesus.

Hymns

TRADITIONAL

- *All hail the power of Jesus' name*
- *May the mind of Christ my Saviour*
- *O God, our help in ages past*
- *O Jesus, I have promised*
- *Praise to the Holiest*

MODERN

- *Christ triumphant*
- *God's Spirit is in my heart*
- *He is Lord, he is Lord*
- *Jesus Christ is waiting*
- *Jesus, name above all names*

Readings

Year A Exodus 17:1-17 or Ezekiel 18:1-4, 25-32; Philippians 2:1-13; Matthew 21:23-32

Year B Esther 7:1-6, 9-10; 9:20-22 or Numbers 11:4-6, 10-16, 24-29; James 5:13-20; Mark 9:38-50

Year C Jeremiah 32:1-3a, 6-15 or Amos 6:1a, 4-7; 1 Timothy 6:6-19; Luke 16:19-31

Confession

Father God, Creator and Life-giver,
we confess before you and one another
the sin which separates us from you.
We repent of our wrongdoing
in thoughtless words and selfish actions,
in seeking status for ourselves
while neglecting the poor and suffering.
We are sorry and ashamed,
and humbly ask your forgiveness and pardon.
By your Spirit increase our faith
and strengthen our will,
that we may walk in your ways
of compassion and care,
through Jesus Christ our Lord. Amen.

Absolution

God our Father,
who knows the deepest desires of our hearts,
hear your prayer of repentance,
grant you pardon and forgiveness
for all your sins,
and guide you on the path
that leads to eternal life in Jesus Christ our Lord.
Amen.

Prayer

Confident that our heavenly Father
will hear us as we pray in faith,
we bring him now those things
which concern and trouble us, saying,
Lord, you are our refuge and fortress;
receive this prayer of faith.

We bring to you the poor of this world –
refugees, street children,
victims of disaster and warfare,
and the exploited or forgotten.
May they find in you hope
when they feel despair,
courage when they feel fearful,
and rejoice in your promise
that they are on your heart.
Lord, you are our refuge and fortress;
receive this prayer of faith.

We bring to you
the wealthy and powerful of this world –

leaders and directors,
economists and accountants,
lawyers and doctors.
May they recognise that all they have
comes from you alone,
using their assets
and discharging their responsibilities
for the good of all people
and the relief of those burdened
by suffering or poverty.
Lord, you are our refuge and fortress;
receive this prayer of faith.

We bring to you
the Christian Church throughout the world –
in freedom or hardship, in strength or weakness,
in joy or sorrow.
May we and all Christian people
demonstrate the love of Christ
in words of wisdom and gentleness
and in acts of compassion and mercy.
Lord, you are our refuge and fortress;
receive this prayer of faith.

We bring to you the suffering and needy,
especially those known to us . . .
May they feel the touch
of your hand on their lives,
healing and restoring,
and upholding them in their time of trouble.
Lord, you are our refuge and fortress;
receive this prayer of faith.

We bring to you our own situations –
decisions to be made, problems to be faced,
challenges to be accepted.
May we live the new life in Christ,
and commit ourselves
wholeheartedly to your kingdom.
Lord, you are our refuge and fortress;
**receive this prayer of faith
in the name of our Saviour Jesus Christ.
Amen.**

All-age address 1

The four Gospels all record Jesus' disputes
and conflicts with the religious authorities in
various degrees of detail. Underlying all of
these was their discomfort with the challenge
Jesus presented, and their refusal to recognise
the source of his authority in his heavenly
Father. They could find an answer for everything, and were assiduous in observing the
Law, but it was all just words. The parable of
the two sons sums it up – the first son may
have challenged his father's instruction, but
eventually he did what was required of him,
unlike his brother, who doubtless made an
immediate impression with his apparent
willingness, but never got round to doing
what he said he would. Like that father, God
wants to see his children bearing fruit for him,
not just uttering fine words. This outline aims
to stress that actions speak louder than words,
and requires only a few previously briefed
volunteers and a minimal amount of
preparation, involving three simple written
instructions placed in an envelope and sealed.

1) The first envelope could be given to a
young child. It should contain a simple and
instantly achievable instruction, for example:
'Fetch me a glass of water.' You're unlikely
to get a refusal (unless you organise it first!)
but persuade your volunteer not to go
straightaway, so that you can highlight the
significance of doing as well as saying.
While the errand is being completed, explain
that such instructions are uncomplicated,
and it's easy to say, 'Yes, of course', without
then quite getting round to it.

2) The second envelope is best given to an
adult, and the instruction here should have
wider implications, such as, 'Obey the
Highway Code'. Ask your volunteer whether
or not it's important to adhere to every last
instruction in it, and then find out whether
they actually do so! Explain that these
instructions aren't for the benefit of one
person but to keep all road-users safe.
Unfortunately, we don't always keep to the
Highway Code as we should, whether
through carelessness, over-confidence, or
simple forgetfulness.

3) The third envelope contains an instruction
that no one could hope to fulfil – 'Sort out
the problem of Third World debt', for
example. It doesn't lie within the power of
just one person to achieve such a thing.
Most people will agree that 'something

needs to be done', but that's not the same as doing it. It's easier to discuss than to tackle, and on our own we may feel we can do nothing. However, we all have a responsibility to work together to make a difference.

Round these points off by reiterating Jesus' words. If we obey someone, we recognise their authority, but if we say we'll do so and then fail to, we're also guilty of hypocrisy. This was what Jesus showed up in the religious people's attitude. As James said, we must be doers of the word as well as hearers.

All-age address 2

Jesus' hearers must have been very struck, not to say disconcerted, by his refusal to let them 'sit on the fence'. However, John and some of the other disciples went a bit over the top when they saw someone they didn't know casting out demons in Jesus' name. Jesus wanted them to realise that anything done in his name would be accepted, regardless of which group the person doing it belonged to. Our actions, as well as our words, give away whose side we're on. This outline (written just before the 1998 World Cup!) looks at this from the point of view of a football supporter. (If you find football tedious, it might be possible to use other sports as an example, though few have as wide an appeal). Beforehand you'll need to acquire a scarf, baseball cap or shirt in the colours of your chosen team.

1) Start by reading out a few of the previous day's scores from the newspaper. It's likely that there'll be some expression of approval at certain results, so follow this up if necessary with a comment such as 'It's obvious who they support'. Say that many people claim to support a particular team when what they mean is that they follow its results. Their support is theoretical and gets no further than pleasure if the team wins.

2) Now ask what evidence there might be of more practical support. Someone will suggest scarves and caps, so produce some at this point, asking for the colours to be identified. Now it can be seen which side someone's on (dress a volunteer up at this point).

3) Scarves and hats are only on the surface. What matters is not looking like a supporter but actually being one. Ask how you can tell whether someone's a genuine supporter. The probable reaction will be 'They go to all the matches'. Now the support isn't just in words, or on the surface, but expressed by encouraging and cheering when the players are in action. The most fanatical supporters organise their whole life around their team's activities.

Conclude by developing these points in terms of Jesus' teaching. The man who John didn't recognise was still on his side, and demonstrating this practically by driving out demons. He didn't even need to do that much – Jesus pointed out that even giving someone a cup of cold water in his name is enough. But the support must be more than nice words or superficial gestures. Our lives must be centred around Jesus Christ himself and directed at living for him.

All-age address 3

The parable of Dives and Lazarus deals with rather more than money and charitable giving. Luke includes it at this point because of its obvious connection with the parable of the shrewd manager in the preceding verses. What happens to us in the next life depends entirely on the way we live in this one, and it's our responsibility to live in accordance with God's will right now, before it's too late. There's no doubt that Jesus' words were aimed at the wealthy and materialistic Pharisees, whose lifestyle emphasised the difference between them and the poor, on whom they looked down. By disregarding so blatantly God's instructions about how to treat the poor, they were living only for the present, complacently assuming that God would have to accept them. In contrast, Jesus uses the poor as a picture of the truly pious, who have their place in heaven. In fact, the contrast between Dives and Lazarus couldn't be greater, either in this life or the next, and the contrast forms the basis of this outline address. Preparation involves finding suitable 'before and after' pictures of people and places.

1) You'll need two pictures of someone who was very famous twenty or thirty years ago, one as they were then and one as they look now (colour supplements and general magazines are always a useful source). Start with the older picture and see if anyone recognises who it is. Then show everyone the more recent picture and ask what's changed about the person. Suggestions will probably include greyer or maybe less hair, an older looking face, different hairstyle, beard shaved off and so on. Time certainly makes a difference to the way we look, and, like it or not, our bodies don't improve with age!

2) Now find pictures of a room before and after redecoration – many magazines run articles along these lines. As before, start off with the earlier picture, and seek suggestions as to what might be done to improve it. Then display the later picture, asking whether or not they think it's an improvement. This is all a matter of taste, but the decorator/interior designer needs to have a clear idea of what the room will look like when finished.

3) Finally, show a picture of a town destroyed by wartime bombing, followed by one after it was rebuilt. Again, the newer version may not appeal to everyone, but the planners needed a clear vision of what they wanted to achieve to give that town a new life after its destruction.

Conclude by pointing out that the way we live now will be conditioned by what we think the next life will be like. For those who follow the way of Jesus, their clear picture of God's kingdom and his rule in their lives will enable them to see that their place in heaven depends not on superficial religiosity or a human idea of 'good taste', but on a life lived in accordance with God's will and in the service of others, most of all the poor.

PROPER 22

Sunday between 2nd and 8th October inclusive

This Sunday's readings are by no means the easiest in the Gospels. In Year A we have Jesus' parable of the tenants, as described by Matthew; in Year B, Mark's account of Jesus' teaching on divorce and the place of small children in the kingdom. The passage from Luke 17 in Year C consists of two short parables, about faith and the duties of servants. All-age worship probably isn't the ideal context for a discussion about divorce, given the complexity of the issues it raises and the enormous range of views to be encountered, so the second outline address, dealing with faith, can be used for both the Year B and C Gospels.

Hymns

TRADITIONAL

- *Have faith in God, my heart*
- *It fell upon a summer day*
- *O Lord, my God*
- *We have a gospel to proclaim*
- *Will your anchor hold*

MODERN

- *Father, I place into your hands*
- *I believe in Jesus*
- *Peace, perfect peace, is the gift*
- *The Lord is my light*
- *We will lay our burden down*

Readings

Year A   Exodus 20:1-4, 7-9, 12-20 or
              Isaiah 5:1-7; Philippians 3:4b-14;
              Matthew 21:33-46
Year B   Job 1:1; 2:1-10 or Genesis 2:18-24;
              Hebrews 1:1-4; 2:5-12; Mark 10:2-16
Year C   Lamentations 1:1-6 or
              Habakkuk 1:1-4; 2:1-4;
              2 Timothy 1:1-14; Luke 17:5-10

Confession

We kneel before our heavenly Father
in penitence for our sins,
yet confident of his forgiveness, saying,
Lord, forgive the sins of your people,
and grant us your salvation.

For living according to human wisdom
rather than in the light of your presence,
Lord, forgive the sins of your people,
and grant us your salvation.

For pursuing our own selfish desires
rather than the paths of righteousness,
Lord, forgive the sins of your people,
and grant us your salvation.

For doing what pleases us
rather than your holy will,
Lord, forgive the sins of your people,
and grant us your salvation.

For seeing only the things of this world
rather than recognising your Son as our Saviour,
Lord, forgive the sins of your people,
**and grant us your salvation,
through Jesus Christ our Lord. Amen.**

Absolution

God, who turns away no one
who comes to him in repentance and faith,
have mercy on you,
pardon and forgive you for all your sins,
and bring you back to his welcoming presence,
through Christ our Lord. Amen.

Prayer

We come before our merciful God,
conscious of the weakness of our faith
but trusting his promise
to hear us and answer, saying,
Accept the prayer of our heart, Lord,
and answer it in your love.

Merciful God, you know the needs
of your Church here in . . .
and throughout the world.
In the weakness of confusion and disunity
may your strength be shown;

in the face of apathy and hostility
may your Gospel be proclaimed;
in the bustle of life
may your peace and love be experienced.
Accept the prayer of our heart, Lord,
and answer it in your love.

Merciful God, you know the needs
of this world and its suffering people –
victims of natural disaster
or man-made catastrophe,
of political instability or local conflict,
of crime or violence,
of exploitation or neglect.
In the pain and despair
may your compassion be revealed
and your love spread abroad.
Accept the prayer of our heart, Lord,
and answer it in your love.

Merciful God, you know the needs
of our local community –
its schools and colleges,
its health centres and places of care,
its businesses and homes,
its unemployed and disaffected members.
In the joy and sorrow of the daily round,
may your good news shine out.
Accept the prayer of our heart, Lord,
and answer it in your love.

Merciful God, you know the needs
of our families and loved ones,
and those in our church family.
We remember especially . . .
In their distress or discomfort, grief or anxiety,
may the presence of your Spirit, the Comforter,
go beside them
to bring healing and guidance.
Accept the prayer of our heart, Lord,
and answer it in your love.

Merciful God, you know each of us
and hear our prayers
even before we put them into words.
Meet us at our point of need
and take us on to where you have called us.
Accept the prayer of our heart, Lord,
and answer it in your love,
that your will may be done
and your kingdom come,
through Jesus Christ our Lord. Amen.

All-age address 1

Jesus' parable of the wicked tenants is a clear anticipation of his impending death at the hands of the Jewish authorities, who understood only too well the point he was making and started to lay plans to curtail his 'subversive' teaching. They had consistently refused to listen to God's voice through the prophets and the Law, using the Scriptures simply to bolster their position in the community and oppress everyone else. In rejecting the Son they were rejecting the Father, and in grave danger of losing their place in the kingdom. Most of today's church-goers wouldn't see themselves as rejecting Jesus, and it's true that 'fashionable' church-going is a thing of the past in many places. However, every Christian needs a reminder that what we claim to be in words we must reflect in our daily lives. This outline address puts the spotlight on why we reject certain aspects of the Christian faith. It needs some prior preparation.

1) Before the service, dissolve a pinch of mixed herbs with water in a small bowl. Start by asking what sort of foods people dislike and why, and after the usual replies of coconut, almond, Stilton cheese and so on, invite someone to taste your concoction without mentioning its ingredients. Even the smallest amount on a teaspoon will create a grimace! Offer a drink of water to remove the taste and explain that we reject some foods because we don't like their flavour. However, we can't put aside the parts of the Christian faith that we find not to our liking.

2) Brief two volunteers beforehand, the first to abuse the other verbally. The second responds by walking away and rejecting the offender (ensure that their language remains acceptable!). If people hurt or insult us, our natural response is to shut them out of our circle of friends and reject them. But sometimes we reject people not because they're being rude but because they challenge the way we think or do things. Jesus was never abusive, but his words were challenging and the authorities found it easier to try and get rid of him than to face the challenge.

3) Now show a picture of a Rottweiler or Dobermann (assuming you wouldn't want to bring in a live example!), and ask how people would react if they saw one at close quarters. Many will say they'd get away as quickly as possible from a close encounter of this kind, though you should emphasise that most dogs, even large breeds, are very rarely vicious. Unfortunately, a few well-publicised cases mean that we react negatively in case there is a risk. Fear often provokes rejection. Some of Jesus' contemporaries were afraid of him and of his popularity with the ordinary poor folk, so they rejected him and his words without thinking any further.

Finish by pointing out how easy it is to reject the bits of Jesus' message that make us uncomfortable or worried, in case he makes a difference to the way we live. No one coming to church is likely to dismiss Jesus out of hand, but what he's looking for are lives which are fruitful for his kingdom. Our faith must be more than good words.

All-age address 2

Faith is a term with a variety of meanings. Some people will use it to refer to a religious belief system, others non-religiously to describe a positive or optimistic outlook on life. Many more will see those with faith as having some belief in an after-life, while others may go further, thinking of it as a conviction that life has a purpose or even a detailed plan. Christians might speak of 'coming to faith', referring to an initial decision or act of commitment to Christianity, but Jesus is talking about an underlying attitude towards God which fundamentally affects the way Christians live – having come to faith, we're then committed to 'living by faith'. This outline address looks at life situations which require us to act in faith, and parallels these with Christian faith.

1) There are many simple actions you can use to demonstrate faith – sitting on a chair is possibly the easiest to stage, but if you're feeling adventurous, ask a child to jump off the pulpit step so that you can catch them, or stand a child in the middle of a ring of four people, and ask them to fall, knowing they'll be caught. Faith has to contain a large element of trust to be effective.

2) Another good example is public transport. Produce a timetable for local trains or buses, saying that you'll be travelling this week, and read out a departure time for your destination. Explain that you have sufficient faith to believe the claim of the transport company that they'll be running this service at the right time. Faith also contains an element of belief and confidence – because this has worked successfully in the past it should do so again. Poor experiences soon lead to a lack of faith. Our faith in God is well-founded on our experience of his goodness and love.

3) Finally, ask your organist or music group leader to change the next hymn (having warned them in advance of your intentions). Having agreed this, point out that your faith in their ability and willingness was sufficient to believe they'd respond favourably. Of course, the ultimate test of faith in a relationship is marriage. Similarly our increasing knowledge of God leads us to trust him as our heavenly Father ever more fully, just as a small child will trust its parent.

PROPER 23

Sunday between 9th and 15th October inclusive

This Sunday's Gospel readings are all well-known passages. Year A brings us Matthew's recounting of the parable of the great wedding feast, and Year B Mark's description of a rich young man who came to see Jesus. For Year C, Luke provides Jesus' miraculous healing of ten lepers, only one of whom returned to give thanks.

Hymns

TRADITIONAL

- *Faithful Shepherd, feed me*
- *Father, hear the prayer we offer*
- *In our day of thanksgiving*
- *Songs of thankfulness and praise*
- *The Lord's my shepherd*

MODERN

- *Give thanks with a grateful heart*
- *God is good*
- *I, the Lord of sea and sky*
- *In the Lord I'll be ever thankful*
- *Oh! Oh! Oh! how good is the Lord*

Readings

Year A Exodus 32:1-14 or Isaiah 25:1-9; Philippians 4:1-9; Matthew 22:1-14
Year B Job 23:1-9, 16-17 or Amos 5:6-7, 10-15; Hebrews 4:12-16; Mark 10:17-31
Year C Jeremiah 29:1, 4-7 or 2 Kings 5:1-3, 7-15c; 2 Timothy 2:8-15; Luke 17:11-19

Confession

Eternal Father, you graciously invite us
to share in the joy of your kingdom,
but we confess that we have turned our backs
on your generosity,
resisted your kindness,
and chosen to follow our own desires.
Forgive all our sins,
pardon our pride and rebellion,

and restore us to the fellowship of your table,
for the sake of your Son,
our Saviour Jesus Christ. Amen.

Absolution

Our loving God,
who welcomes all who turn to him
in penitence and faith,
have mercy on you, forgive all your sins
and bring you into the eternal joy of the new life
which comes through Jesus Christ,
our risen Lord. Amen.

Prayer

Our heavenly Father
invites us to his eternal feast,
not because we deserve it
but because he wants us to be present.
We respond to his love and kindness, saying,
Generous God,
make us one with you.

Heavenly Father, you call us
with all Christian people
to be members of your kingdom.
Bless and guide your Church,
local and worldwide,
as it worships and serves you,
enable it to bring your transforming love
to this needy world,
and help it to realise the unity
which it has in Christ our Lord.
Especially we pray . . .
Generous God,
make us one with you.

Heavenly Father,
there is room in your kingdom
for those on the edges of society –
the homeless and unwanted,
the poor and downtrodden,
the ignored and ill-treated.
Sustain and give hope to those whose lives
are filled with pain and despair,
especially . . .
Generous God,
make us one with you.

Heavenly Father,
there are signs of your kingdom
even in war-torn, distressed places,
where fear and hardship overshadow life,
especially . . .
Give comfort to the suffering,
release to the oppressed,
and strength to those who work
to bring relief and peace.
Generous God,
make us one with you.

Heavenly Father, the light of your kingdom
shines in every kind of darkness –
illness of mind or body,
anxiety or grief, crisis or burden.
We remember especially . . .
Reach out with your healing hand
to bring them consolation, wholeness and joy.
Generous God,
make us one with you.

Heavenly Father, we pray that in our lives
your kingdom will come and your will be done,
as we serve you in one another
and look forward
to your promise of eternal life.
Generous God,
make us one with you,
both now and until that day
when we will rejoice in your presence for ever.
Amen.

All-age address 1

There's no better demonstration of Jesus' sense of humour than the parable of the great wedding feast. Responding to a particularly pious question from someone decidedly 'holier than thou', he has a field-day with the silly excuses to show up the stupidity of those who, in rejecting him, were rejecting their heavenly Father. The context today may be rather different, but people still make all kinds of excuses for not committing themselves to the way of Christ. Invitations are a good focus for an all-age address, not least because they demand a response. Some advance preparation is needed. Draw up large-scale invitation cards to three different events – a garden party, an important business lunch and a celebrity banquet. The first two should be elaborate and flashy, looking important and glamorous, with the third relatively plain. You'll need a volunteer to hold these up for all to see, and you'll also need an invented menu for each, which can be read out. Before you start, show the congregation all three invitations and conduct a quick survey of which event they might go to.

1) The first menu is in French (if possible), so that it sounds pretty impressive until translated into English. A good list of thoroughly unpleasant tastes (dishwater soup of the day, fat and gristle pie, for example) will be guaranteed to provoke a disgusted response! Cap this by suggesting that guests will have to pay £80 a head for the privilege, and underline the quality of the invitation card. Ask the congregation what excuses they could make to avoid going to this – a diplomatic illness or 'back trouble' are likely suggestions, followed maybe by double-booking or a prior engagement. Point out that people often make excuses to avoid something they think will be distasteful or unpleasant.

2) The second 'menu' should be very similar to the first, though emphasise that this is a business lunch, so expenses will be limited and hard work required. Again, find out what excuses people might use to get out of this invitation, while commending the artwork and high quality production of the invitation itself. Point out that most of us use an excuse to avoid something like this which seems boring and onerous.

3) The final 'menu' should be as mouthwatering as possible, including dishes which will appeal to children such as Big Macs or ice-cream. Add to this by saying that there'll be lots of well-known celebrities there too, and it's all completely free of charge. No one's going to make excuses to turn down this one, even though the invitation itself is a bit plain and uninteresting at first sight.

Finish by saying that many people turn down God's invitation to be part of his kingdom because at first glance it seems less attractive than some other options. So, not realising what they're missing out on, they make their excuses – 'not enough time', 'too much else to do', 'when I'm older', 'I want to spend time with my family'. But, if we look more closely, we realise that for all their immediate appeal, the attractions of this world don't live up to their initial impact and soon become dull or even repulsive. In contrast, the more we experience of God's kingdom, the more we realise it has to offer.

All-age address 2

'The cost of discipleship – only £2.95', read the slogan on the bookstall. If only! Few congregations have exceptionally wealthy members today, but you don't need to be a millionaire to suffer from the same problem as the rich young man who came to Jesus one day. We aren't entirely clear about his motives, but he was genuine enough. Devout and God-fearing, faithful to the Law and sincerely wanting to please God, the biggest obstacle preventing him from following Jesus was that he had too much to lose. Not that Jesus was bothered about wealth *per se*, but he knew that it could engender attitudes which form a barrier to keep God at a safe distance. However much we may complain about being hard up, those same attitudes are just as prevalent now and can have a significant effect on church life. This address outline needs some preparation in order to bring out the blocks which prevent so many people from coming to Jesus and following him. You'll need four boxes of different sizes so they can fit over each other to be removed one at a time, and a small wrapped 'treasure' which will fit into the smallest box.

1) The largest box covers all the others, and on it is written 'Money and possessions'. Like the young man, most of us hang on to what we have, afraid of losing it. This fear is probably the biggest single factor in preventing people from being committed to following Christ. Our society promotes ownership as a cardinal rule of life, but this militates against exercising faith and gives

the idea that this life is the only one that matters. It's vital to stress that wrong attitudes to money and possessions aren't the preserve of the really wealthy – however little we may think we have, we can still allow it to come between us and God.

2) The next box should say 'Time'. After money, the next largest problem for most of us is time, and for the same reason – we never have enough! It can be very demanding to balance all our priorities and give the right amount of time to our work or studies, families or friends, church or social activities. When we feel tired after a day's work, when it feels as though everyone is pressurising us, when we wonder how to fit everything in, God easily gets squeezed out.

3) The third box has the caption 'Other people'. This can be another distraction of major proportions. It may be that one other person (or group of people) becomes more important to us than God, but equally we can become so obsessed with someone who upsets or annoys us that we can't think of anything else. Families can also be unhealthily possessive and demanding. Human relationships are complex, even unfathomable, and can profoundly affect us in all sorts of ways, taking our attention away from our relationship with Christ.

4) The final box says 'Self'. We can spend so much time, energy and even money on ourselves that there's nothing left for anyone or anything else. It's right and proper to attend to health problems or personal relationships and issues, but not to the extent that God is shut out and we're unable to think of anything else. This may be the least obvious obstacle to following the way of Christ, but the hardest to deal with.

At the end you come across the 'treasure' (such as a small gift-wrapped bar of chocolate), and as you do so, point out that the rewards of the Christian life depend on us being willing to remove the obstacles which keep us away from them.

All-age address 3

Saying thank you is something all children learn almost as soon as they can talk. So it's important to recognise that Luke didn't include this incident in order to teach about good manners, but to highlight one man's response to the transforming power of Jesus. The leper who returns to Jesus to give thanks for his healing finds his life transformed, not just because he's been cured of a socially unacceptable disease but even more because his grateful response opens up a new relationship with the Saviour. This outline address, therefore, puts less emphasis on etiquette (though acknowledging the importance of expressing gratitude) than on the relationship which lies behind giving and receiving.

1) Start by offering a member of the congregation a wrapped sweet (Roses chocolates are quite useful as they have been marketed as a way of saying thank you). The response will either be 'No, thank you' or more likely 'Yes, please – thank you'. Thanking someone for their generosity or consideration is an essential part of our relationship with them. If they've given something, however small, it's a sign that they value their relationship with us; our thanks indicates that we also value it.

2) The rest of the address is a simple mnemonic on the word 'thankful'. Each letter is also the initial letter of a word referring to a gift of God for which we should be thankful. A card with each letter and word on it could be held up by a volunteer.

T – Time. Jesus gave the lepers his time and attention, and God has given us the gift of time to use for his glory.

H – Healing. Jesus gave the leper healing from the condition which separated him from other people. He heals us of the things which separate us from each other and God, as well as illness or pain.

A– Answer. Jesus answered their cry for help and mercy. He always answers those who cry to him in distress and sadness.

N – New life. Healing meant a whole new life for the lepers, as they could mix with other people once again. We too have new life in the Spirit through Jesus' death and resurrection.

K – Kindness. The lepers hadn't earned Jesus' act of kindness. God shows us his love and mercy not because we deserve it but because of his kindness.

F – Families and friends. We may not always feel thankful for them, but life would be lonely and frightening on our own. God the Father, Son and Holy Spirit live in relationship, and God created us likewise, to relate to him and to each other.

U – Unlimited joy. Imagine how the lepers must have felt to know they were healed! This isn't superficial jollity but a deep sense of how much God has done, how much we owe him, and how much we want to share that with other people.

L – Love. Jesus' motivation was only ever love. The leper who returned was the one who recognised this and continued the relationship. God's love dwells in our lives and transforms them if we respond to it and allow him to make us more like him.

PROPER 24

Sunday between 16th and 22nd October inclusive

Today's reading for Year A from Matthew's Gospel is the well-known passage in which Jesus distinguishes between divine and human authority, sidestepping a trap set for him by his opponents. Year B's Gospel reading from Mark depicts James and John trying to get the best place in heaven. In Year C, Luke retells Jesus' parable of the persistent widow.

Hymns

TRADITIONAL

- *For the healing of the nations*
- *Forth in the peace of Christ we go*
- *Forth in thy name, O Lord, I go*
- *Thy hand, O God, has guided*
- *What a friend we have in Jesus*

MODERN

- *From heaven you came*
- *Jesus is Lord*
- *Meekness and majesty*
- *Restore, O Lord*
- *Stay with me*

Readings

Year A   Exodus 33:12-23 or Isaiah 45:1-7;
         1 Thessalonians 1:1-10;
         Matthew 22:15-22
Year B   Job 38:1-7 (34-41) or Isaiah 53:4-12;
         Hebrews 5:1-10; Mark 10:35-45
Year C   Jeremiah 31:27-34 or Genesis 32:22-31;
         2 Timothy 3:14-4:5; Luke 18:1-8

Confession

Lord, you are a forgiving God,
slow to anger yet swift to show mercy.
We confess with sorrow
our failure to acknowledge your lordship
over our lives,
our concern with our own well-being,
and our lack of faith.
Pardon all our sins, we ask you,
blot out our offences,

and by your Spirit fit us to be worthy servants
of your kingdom,
through our Saviour Jesus Christ. Amen.

Absolution

Almighty God, whose arms are ever open
to receive those who come to him
in penitence and faith,
have mercy on you,
forgive all your wrongdoing
and assure you of his eternal faithfulness
and goodness,
through Jesus Christ our Lord. Amen.

Prayer

We come before our Father in heaven,
offering him our worship and praise,
and laying at his feet the burdens of our heart.
Lord, teach us always to pray
and never to lose heart.

We think of the Church
in every part of the world,
enduring opposition and persecution,
confronting evil and corruption,
challenging cynicism and apathy.
We pray for all mission initiatives
and efforts to share the good news,
especially . . .
When we feel disheartened,
give us courage to persevere.
Lord, teach us always to pray
and never to lose heart.

We think of governments and all in authority,
stretched by economic and social problems,
crime and violence, war and famine.
We pray for politicians and civic leaders
as they make laws and decisions, especially . . .
When we feel disillusioned,
give us a vision of your eternal kingdom.
Lord, teach us always to pray
and never to lose heart.

We think of those whose lives are burdened
with illness, grief, disappointment or insecurity,
whose pilgrimage lies under the dark shadow
of pain and suffering.
We pray for our families and friends,
and anyone we know

who needs the comfort of your presence,
especially . . .
When we feel dispirited,
renew our zeal and inspire our faith.
Lord, teach us always to pray
and never to lose heart.

We think of those whose
earthly pilgrimage is ended
and who are now at rest in you,
especially . . .
We pray that we may hold
their example before us
and follow them in the narrow way
that leads to eternal life.
Lord, teach us always to pray
and never to lose heart,
that one day we may rejoice for ever
in your kingdom of light,
which we ask in the name of your Son,
our Saviour Jesus Christ. Amen.

All-age address 1

The Gospels contain several instances of Jesus'
opponents trying to snare him into saying
something incriminating, which would give
them an excuse to deal with him. On each
occasion he not only avoided the trap, but did
so with such profound insight that he couldn't
be answered. 'Rendering unto Caesar what
belongs to Caesar' is an expression often used
in a secular context, so familiar is it, though
regrettably less people today seem familiar with
rendering to God what is God's. The issue
which underlies Jesus' answer is how to live
as citizens both of this world and of God's
kingdom. It's too complex to tackle in depth in
all-age worship, but this outline aims to provide
a basic understanding both of the tensions
involved and the opportunities available.
It's based on the same principle as the game
'Scruples', and the only preparation needed
is the production of a few 'game cards' with
appropriate questions.

1) The first question is about personal morals.
'A supermarket cashier gives me £10 too
much change, but I only realise this when I
get home. Do I: (a) take it back as soon as
possible? (b) post it back by return? (c) give
it to charity since the firm makes big
profits? (d) keep it?' Two willing members
of the congregation may be happy to give
their verdict on this, but finish by asking
the whole congregation what they think,
ideally by a show of hands. This issue is
quite straightforward, and it's not likely
that (c) or (d) will be supported in a church
context. Christians are called to be good
citizens and deal honestly in every aspect
of their lives.

2) The second question is much more a question of choice. 'I'm thinking about booking
a summer holiday when an appeal is
broadcast for famine victims. Should I: (a)
forget the holiday and give the money I
would have spent to the charity? (b) book
the holiday and give an equal amount to
the charity? (c) book a holiday that costs
half what I was intending to spend and
give the rest to charity? (d) decide my
Christian giving is already organised and
just book the holiday?' In this case there's
no easy right or wrong answer as there
are a number of factors to consider – the
holiday may be essential for family or
health reasons; funds may well be limited;
Christian giving should be an ongoing
activity rather than a 'knee-jerk' response
to need. On the other hand, it would be
wrong as Christians to remain unmoved by
great human need when we're able to make
a significant contribution – Jesus was often
moved by compassion.

3) The third question is more ethical. 'I discover
that my best friend is addicted to drugs,
and stealing in order to finance their habit.
Do I: (a) tell the police at once? (b) warn
him of the possible consequences? (c) tell
his parents or a teacher? (d) ignore it and
assume it's a phase that will pass, and
anyway it's not my business?' This is a very
real problem, and even (d) isn't as clear-
cut as it seems – many youngsters do go
through difficult phases, and we have no
automatic right to interfere in the lives of
others, however much we may disagree with
their actions. Having said that, it would be
wrong not to challenge harmful behaviour,
and the friend may well be unable to control
his addiction on his own, in which case our
help may be invaluable. As Christians we
make decisions based on the best interests of

everyone concerned, though emphasise that we aren't entitled to become judgemental.

4) The last question is specifically Christian: 'I accept a new job for an organisation, which I then discover expects me to compromise my integrity and faith through deceit and financial irregularity. Do I: (a) resign at once? (b) try to carry on the job without being dishonest? (c) explain my concerns to my superiors and risk dismissal? (d) go along with it because the family comes first and the mortgage has to be paid?' Many Christians are familiar with a scenario like this. No one can dispute that families need to be supported, and as Christians we should be good employees. However, no one has authority to condone wrong-doing, still less to command it, and our Christian witness will be seriously impaired if we close our eyes and consciences to what we know is wrong. Faith can sometimes feel very risky, but making a stand may ultimately do far more for God's kingdom than refusing to accept responsibility.

Conclude by pointing out that as Christians there's not usually a conflict between being citizens and members of the kingdom of God. But when we're faced with the choice of obeying wrong instructions or obeying God, our first duty is to the Lord of lords.

All-age address 2

You can use the second outline address for Proper 20 as the basis for one on this week's Gospel from the following chapter of Mark, but after going through the four status symbols, this time bring on a fifth, a bowl of water and a flannel. This was the status symbol that Jesus used (see John 13:1-15), and, as disciples, this symbol of service should be the only one that defines us.

All-age address 3

It seems odd to our culture that Jesus should speak of a persistent widow – perhaps our minds turn more readily to children who never give up with their demands! – but in those days it was probably the only means she had of obtaining justice. The judge is of equal importance to the parable, self-centred and arrogant. Jesus wants his hearers to understand that if a hard-nosed, unsympathetic magistrate can be swayed by a poor but persistent widow, how much more will our heavenly Father listen to those who cry to him for help. The question of unanswered prayer troubles some people greatly (usually because they didn't get the answer they wanted), but this outline tries to promote an understanding of prayer which goes beyond the 'slot machine' concept.

1) Produce a few 'instant' foods or drinks – coffee, custard, cakes, for example. Point out that we can now go to the supermarket and get instant food which needs little or no preparation. We've become very used to this, and we now find it hard to wait for anything – we want it *now*, and as consumers assume that's our right. God, however, isn't a consumer service provider who's obliged to deal with special orders on the spot. He's our eternal Lord and King, and we can't order him about or drag him down to our own level.

2) Next produce a couple of credit cards, explaining that they enable us to 'have now and pay later'. Older members may still remember having to 'save up' for an item they wanted, but today instant gratification is all too easy – though the consequences later on can be disastrous as the debts mount up. God isn't there to provide whatever we want whenever we want it – the so-called 'prosperity gospel' is a gross distortion of the Gospel of Christ.

3) The widow in the parable was asking for justice rather than self-gratification. God will always hear us when we cry to him in real need, or when we pray for others in need. His answer may not be the one we wanted, but we can be sure it will be the best for us, as God will only ever act in our best interests. To conclude, display a few charity leaflets requesting money and support, and indicate that if our prayers are directed towards these needs, we know God will respond in his love.

Proper 25

Sunday between 23rd and 29th October inclusive

We've now reached the final 'Proper' (though your church may use this Sunday to celebrate its Dedication Festival). However, the consecutive Gospel readings continue through to the Sunday before Advent (the new festival of Christ the King, which is covered in *Come to the Feast Book 1*). Matthew's Gospel in Year A brings Jesus' words about the greatest commandment, and his status as the Christ. Mark, in Year B, has the familiar story of blind Bartimaeus. For Year C we have the short but challenging excerpt from Luke about the Pharisee and the publican.

Hymns

TRADITIONAL

- *All hail the power of Jesus' name*
- *Amazing grace*
- *At the name of Jesus*
- *Hail to the Lord's anointed*
- *Just as I am*

MODERN

- *God is good*
- *He is exalted*
- *I'm accepted, I'm forgiven*
- *Open our eyes, Lord*
- *When I feel the touch*

Readings

Year A Deuteronomy 34:1-12 or
Leviticus 19:1-2, 15-18;
1 Thessalonians 2:1-8;
Matthew 22:34-46
Year B Job 42:1-6, 10-17 or Jeremiah 31:7-9;
Hebrews 7:23-28; Mark 10:46-52
Year C Joel 2:23-32 or Ecclesiasticus 35:12-17
or Jeremiah 14:7-10, 19-22;
2 Timothy 4:6-8, 16-18; Luke 18:9-14

Confession

We come into God's holy presence,
aware of our failings and wrongdoing, saying,
Lord, we are truly sorry and repent of our sins;
forgive us and make us whole.

Our actions are too often motivated
by personal concerns
rather than by the needs of others
and the building of your kingdom.
Lord, we are truly sorry and repent of our sins;
forgive us and make us whole.

Our words are too often formed
by our own opinions and interests
rather than by the feelings of others
and the proclamation of your kingdom.
Lord, we are truly sorry and repent of our sins;
forgive us and make us whole.

Our thoughts are too often dominated
by our personal viewpoint
rather than by the well-being of others
and the truth of your kingdom.
Lord, we are truly sorry and repent of our sins;
forgive us and make us whole.

Our lives are too often directed
by selfish ambition
rather than by serving others in Christ's name
and demonstrating the power of his kingdom.
Lord, we are truly sorry and repent of our sins;
forgive us and make us whole,
fill our mouths with your praises
and make us faithful servants,
for the sake of your Son,
our Saviour Jesus Christ. Amen.

Absolution

Our heavenly Father, by whose grace alone
we are worthy to stand before him,
have mercy on you,
forgive all your sins,
free you from guilt,
and set you free to praise and glorify his name,
through Christ our Lord. Amen.

Prayer

We offer thanksgiving and prayers
to our Lord Jesus,
who gave sight to the blind, saying,
Lord, open our eyes to your presence;
help us to walk in your light.

In faith we pray for the Church
in every country and circumstance,
especially . . .
May we and all Christian people
rejoice at your presence in praise and worship,

in fellowship and companionship,
in service and mission.
Lord, open our eyes to your presence;
help us to walk in your light.

In faith we pray for the world's leaders
as they tackle the problems
of famine and poverty,
disaster and crisis, education and health,
especially . . .
May we see your hand at work in the world,
in international affairs, in the community
and in each other.
Lord, open our eyes to your presence;
help us to walk in your light.

In faith we pray for those we know
who are living through times of
illness or depression, uncertainty or burden,
especially . . .
May they know your Spirit
comforting and guiding them
through their trials.
Lord, open our eyes to your presence;
help us to walk in your light.

In faith we pray for those
who have finished their earthly pilgrimage
and now rest in your love,
especially . . .
May their example inspire us to persevere
and continue our walk with you.
Lord, open our eyes to your presence;
help us to walk in your light,
until we rejoice in the eternal day of heaven,
through Jesus Christ our Lord. Amen.

All-age address 1

Jesus was often asked trick questions in the vain hope that he'd say something incriminating. He never did, but that didn't stop the questions coming. Here he's asked about the most important law by a legal 'expert', who should have known better. Jesus' knowledge of the Law is as superior to theirs as is his understanding of the human condition. In response, he throws *them* a question, based on the Law, which not only demonstrates that he knows it as well as they do but also leaves them silent. Their refusal to recognise Jesus as the promised Messiah demonstrably contradicted the Scriptures they claimed to believe in. (This

address outline is similar to the one for the Sunday next before Lent, which celebrates the Transfiguration.)

1) Disfigure a large magazine-sized photo of a well-known personality with moustache, glasses, and so on. As you display it, ask for identification, and point out that the Pharisees were deliberately distorting their image of Jesus so as not to recognise him. Unfortunately for them, too many other people realised who he really was.

2) Play a small section of a tape of someone's voice and see if anyone knows who it is. Sometimes it's the subject matter as much as the qualities of the voice itself which is the giveaway. Jesus certainly had a reputation in Israel, but it was what he taught that showed his authority, not just the way he presented it.

3) Now hold up a large copy of a famous painting and ask who the artist is – often it's obvious just from the subject and style of the painting. We recognise the work even though the person who produced it may well have died many years ago. The Pharisees could have worked out that Jesus was the Christ from what he did as well as what he said, but so determinedly blind were they that they could only think of ways to get rid of him by setting traps. But in answering their silly questions, Jesus demonstrated even more clearly that he was who he claimed to be.

All-age address 2

Most people, if asked, would say they value sight more than any of the other senses. Today we have guide-dogs, braille, and the medical knowledge to prevent at least some blindness, but for Bartimaeus to be unsighted was a life sentence. As with so many others healed by Jesus, he was made whole not just in one area but in every aspect of life. Most important he could live and work normally, no longer feeling the social stigma attached to disability and certain illnesses. For this simple outline you need just two willing volunteers (preferably, though not necessarily, primed in advance) and a blindfold.

1) Tie the blindfold around your first volunteer's eyes, making sure it's effective! Give him an apple (or something similar) and ask him to identify it. A person who can't see has to rely on his other senses to recognise objects.

2) Now ask him what colour it is. Someone blind from birth has no concept of colour – a whole dimension of life is missing.

3) Bring up a friend of the blindfolded volunteer and see if he can be recognised by touch or general shape. Blindness means that parents, spouses and children have to be identified by voice or touch.

4) Turn your volunteer round three times and ask him to find his way to the organ (or wherever is convenient). A blind person can't identify places or distance, and finds his way about either with a trained dog, or by learning to use a white stick.

5) Bartimaeus had an even bigger problem – he couldn't work, and was a social outcast, so his life revolved around begging. No one expected Jesus to bother with him (apart from Bartimaeus himself), so when he responded to the persistent cries for help, some people were surprised, even offended, and tried to dissuade him. But the touch of Jesus' hand transformed Bartimaeus – he could see people, places, objects and colours, and no longer had to endure being marginalised and vulnerable.

Conclude by explaining that Jesus is concerned not just to cure a condition or illness but to transform every part of our lives with his love, so that we can be free to get up and follow him, as Bartimaeus did.

All-age address 3

One of the most besetting of all the human race's sins is surely that of comparing ourselves with each other in the most favourable light. We constantly seek reassurance about our own moral status by trying to denigrate other people's, and while we may focus on typically twentieth-century areas, Jesus perceptively pinpoints the universality of this condition. In this case it was the Pharisees who indulged in spiritual and moral one-upmanship, and, as the parable makes clear, self-righteousness of this kind is the biggest single stumbling-block to membership of God's kingdom. Significantly, the tax collector doesn't dwell mawkishly on his sins and personal inadequacy, but compares himself only with the standards expected of him by God, which he has manifestly failed to attain. This outline aims to pick up on the areas in which we're tempted to compare ourselves with others, and on the areas in which we *should* try to outdo each other. You need to draw a large tree with ten branches, on which you place or draw five rotten and five juicy red apples.

1) The five rotten apples represent the ways in which we like to think of ourselves as superior to others – education, wealth, personal standards, social standing and popularity, and moral viewpoints. (If the picture's large enough write the relevant word on each fruit.) Each of these is self-evident and it's fairly straightforward to think of examples. Our education can easily tempt us to think of ourselves as more knowledgeable or better informed; wealth soon convinces us that we're in favour with God; personal standards are an easy way of putting down anyone who's different to us; social standing persuades us that God thinks better of us than our friends; while on moral viewpoints – well, how many people do you know who think they might have got it wrong?

2) The five desirable fruits are the fruits of the Spirit – love, joy, peace, patience and kindness (you could add others if you've time). In God's kingdom no one is superior or inferior to anyone else. Instead, our thoughts should be about what we can do to improve the lives of other people. All the time we're thinking about ourselves and whether we're better than someone else, we're preventing our lives from being fruitful. As followers of Jesus we're called to bear fruit for his glory.

FOURTH SUNDAY BEFORE ADVENT

Sunday between 30th October
and 5th November inclusive

Many churches will want to keep this Sunday to celebrate All Saints, but if you choose to keep All Saints on 1st November, the lectionary continues on this Sunday with the consecutive Gospel readings (although the four Sundays before Advent don't include an alternative Old Testament lesson). In Year A we come to Matthew's account of the 'Little Apocalypse', Jesus' description of the 'last days'. The Year B reading from Mark is Jesus' answer to the question about the greatest commandment. In Year C Luke tells of Zacchaeus, the tax collector's life-changing encounter with Jesus.

Hymns

TRADITIONAL

- *Come down, O Love divine*
- *Jesu, thou joy of loving hearts*
- *Mine eyes have seen the glory*
- *O happy day*
- *Thy way, not mine, O Lord*

MODERN

- *Father God, I wonder*
- *O Lord, your tenderness*
- *Spirit of the living God*
- *The Spirit lives to set us free*
- *Wait for the Lord*

Readings

Year A   Micah 3:5-12; 1 Thessalonians 2:9-13; Matthew 24:1-14

Year B   Deuteronomy 6:1-9; Hebrews 9:11-14; Mark 12:28-34

Year C   Isaiah 1:10-18; 2 Thessalonians 1:1-12; Luke 19:1-10

Confession

Lord Jesus, risen Master,
we come before you burdened with guilt,
weighed down by our sins.
We are ashamed of our wrongdoing,
and long to be set free.
Forgive us all that is past,
and in your mercy take away our heavy load.
Restore and renew our lives, we pray,
and release us from the oppression of sin
into the joy of your salvation,
for your name's sake. Amen.

Absolution

Almighty God, who forgives all
who confess their sins in penitence and faith,
have mercy on you,
cleanse you from every kind of wrong,
make you faithful in following him,
and keep you in eternal life,
through his Son, our Saviour Jesus Christ.
Amen.

Prayer

The presence of the risen Jesus
transforms every person and situation.
Confident of his power and love,
we bring him our requests and concerns, saying,
Gracious Lord,
in your mercy hear us.

We ask you to transform your Church
by your Spirit.
Take away barriers of suspicion and fear,
fill our hearts with your joy and praise,
and unite us in your service.
Bless our work of mission and evangelism,
especially . . .
Gracious Lord,
in your mercy hear us.

We ask you to transform this world
by your power.
Give wisdom and courage to world leaders,
hope and encouragement
to the downtrodden and vulnerable,
peace and tranquillity
to lives wrecked by warfare and conflict.

Bless all aid-workers, peacemakers
and decision-takers, especially . . .
Gracious Lord,
in your mercy hear us.

We ask you to transform with your love
the lives of those overwhelmed by pain or fear.
Give healing and wholeness
to the sick in body and mind,
comfort and peace to the dying,
and hope to the fearful and weary.
Bless any we know who are suffering,
especially . . .
Gracious Lord,
in your mercy hear us.

We ask you to transform us
so that we become more like you.
Touch us with your presence,
restore us by your grace,
and equip us to serve you faithfully
in whatever task you call us to.
Gracious Lord,
in your mercy hear us,
and answer these prayers
for the sake of your Son,
Jesus Christ our Lord. Amen.

All-age address 1

There have always been wild theories about
the end of the world, especially at the turn of
a century or millennium. Jesus' words, as
recorded by the evangelists, have been applied
to all kinds of world events with absolute
certainty, even by Christians, in the firm belief
that his return in glory is imminent. We can
hardly blame the disciples for their question,
but nowhere does the Bible encourage us to
indulge in eschatological crystal-ball-gazing –
'even the Son of Man does not know the day
or hour'. At the same time, however, Jesus
wanted his followers to be real about the way
things would go, to teach them how to recognise
the 'signs of the times', and to be encouraged
in their discipleship. This outline aims to avoid
speculation and concentrate attention instead
on signs. Four large-scale drawings (or OHP
slides) of road signs are needed, to be displayed
at the appropriate time.

1) The first sign is the one for a slippery road.
Begin by asking the drivers present if any
of them have ever skidded their car. Sometimes a road surface can deceive us by
looking secure, or a bend can be sharper
than we think. We need the sign to warn us
that our eyes might be fooled. Jesus told
his disciples that many people would be
deceived by impostors, who would claim to
be him and lead them astray. It's easy to be
taken in by clever talkers, and Christians
need to make sure that what they hear
measures up to the teaching of Jesus.

2) The second sign is for low-flying aircraft.
Point out that the sign isn't to warn of a real
danger – it's unlikely that a plane will land
on the roadway by mistake. But a driver
could be alarmed by the sudden noise of an
aircraft, and possibly cause an accident as a
result. There are plenty of things to alarm
us in the world, such as wars, natural
disasters and poverty. However, they aren't
in themselves signs that the end is about
to happen.

3) The third sign is for roadworks – and for
most drivers that means a frustrating
experience! There's hard work involved in
the Christian life, too, and we can be
tempted to give up, especially when we
encounter difficulties or opposition. Jesus
knew his followers would face plenty of
both, which is why he encouraged them to
'stand firm to the end'.

4) The final sign says 'End', a welcome sight
after miles of cones and contraflow! Jesus
promises that our journey of faith will end
in the joy of heaven, and, before that, all the
peoples of the world will hear the good
news of the kingdom. The journey won't
always be easy, but we know that Jesus will
travel alongside, guiding and protecting us.

All-age address 2

Getting priorities in the right order is a task
everyone can identify with! Jesus' questioner
on this occasion was clearly trying to set a
trap, but he highlights a problem which can be

on one level simply practical or on another seriously ethical. It may be nothing more complex than choosing which of two events to attend; it may also involve choosing between two people in a way which is bound to hurt one of them; at worst, for Christians, there may be an impossible moral choice between two courses of action, neither of which would be desirable. Context and conscience will both play their part in deciding how to handle these problems, but this outline aims simply to provide an indication of how we might go about establishing our priorities as Christians. Four large sheets of paper with three 'multiple choice' answers need to be prepared in advance.

1) Ask the younger children which should have the priority: (a) watching a TV programme; (b) playing in the garden; (c) tidying the bedroom. None of these have a moral element, but if parents have asked for tidying up to be done, obeying their request must take priority over other things which we might prefer to do. This is a simple way to obey Jesus' law of love.

2) Now ask the teenagers for their priority from a choice of: (a) revising for GCSEs; (b) helping parents mow the lawn; (c) keeping a friend company by watching a video with them. This is tougher! All of these are constructive, even if revision is most important in the longer term. Helping around the house is also important, as is being a good friend, and the decision in this case will depend on the immediate context. Jesus' law of love needs to be applied thoughtfully – revision shouldn't be used as an excuse for laziness or unhelpfulness, nor should being a good friend become an excuse for not working or helping.

3) Ask the young parents next which of the following they would regard as top priority: (a) working hard to earn enough money for a nice house or car; (b) spending quality time with the children; (c) enjoying an active social life. Again this is hard, as all three are good in themselves. Work is part of God's created order, as are families and friends. But if work dominates too much, then families and friends suffer, while too

much socialising will affect family life and performance at work. We have to demonstrate the love of Jesus in all those areas.

4) Finally, ask the older members of the congregation for their number one choice out of: (a) making sure they have an adequate pension; (b) providing for their children and grandchildren; (c) making the most of the later years of life while still fit to do so. Again, these are all good in themselves – the question is which should take priority and when. Sensible financial provision, care for the family, and living life to the full all have their place, but not if one excludes the others. Jesus' law of love indicates that we should live in such a way that as many people benefit as possible.

Conclude by saying that the first priority for all Christians is God himself. That doesn't necessarily mean attending lots of meetings at church, but it does mean that God and his kingdom will be at the forefront of the way we use our money and time, and organise our lives.

All-age address 3

Zacchaeus is one of the most memorable characters in the New Testament. Not that we know a great deal about him, but few people demonstrate more effectively the transforming power of the Lord Jesus. As a tax collector for a hated occupying power he was hardly going to be at the top of many people's party invitation list, but, to make it worse, he used his powers to line his own pocket at the expense of his fellow-countrymen. Most people would have viewed him as 'beyond the pale'. We've no idea what drew Zacchaeus to Jesus, or why he wanted to see him without being seen himself, but the turn of events must have given him a severe shock! Others were less impressed by Jesus giving his time to such a dubious character, but, even in their disapproval of Jesus' choice of company, they couldn't deny the subsequent change. A few years ago a very popular toy was the Transformer, a seemingly innocuous car which, with a few strategic twists, could be turned into a fearsome robot – you could barely recognise it as the same lump of plastic! Zacchaeus was still recognisably the same person after Jesus called him out of his tree, he hadn't undergone a personality refit but no one could believe that this fraudulent, exploitative, scheming little man was now so different.

1) Jesus transformed his *sadness*. A box of tissues is a good visual aid here, though it's unlikely that Zacchaeus would ever have been so overtly emotional. Deep down he was miserable and afraid. His wealth had left him with few friends and many enemies – the tree was a useful hiding place as well as a vantage point. But when Jesus stopped and asked him to climb down, he didn't seem to mind who saw him! Jesus' perfect love 'casts out fear'.

2) Jesus dealt with his *guilt*. Because Zacchaeus faced up to his wrongdoing he was set free from guilt and from the inward damage caused by its fearful, furtive secrecy. A symbol of punishment, such as a cane, would reinforce this point, though it would be wise to point out that past rather than present generations of schoolchildren were afraid of this punishment! Once guilt has been brought out into the open and dealt with, it no longer has any power to create fear or harm.

3) Jesus transformed his *lifestyle*. Filofaxes, floppy disks, cheque books are all good symbols of the controlling factors in life today. Zacchaeus' life was totally dominated by his money-making, but his riches didn't do anything for the quality of his life. By choosing to follow Jesus, his whole life was transformed because these other factors no longer controlled it.

4) Jesus transformed his *relationships*. Friendless, lonely Zacchaeus no longer had to live in fear of the consequences of his behaviour. By putting matters right with those he'd exploited, he removed the major blockage between himself and other people. Only his encounter with Jesus could have achieved such a change. Zacchaeus was still recognisably the same person, but now his life was positive in direction and had a purpose.

THIRD SUNDAY BEFORE ADVENT

Sunday between 6th and 12th November inclusive

In most years Remembrance Sunday will fall on the Third Sunday before Advent, and many churches will want to focus on the issues that raises. However, readings are provided in the new lectionary for those churches where Remembrance doesn't dominate the main service, although they fit in well with that theme. In Year A we read Jesus' parable of the ten bridesmaids, for which an outline address is provided here. For Mark's account of the start of Jesus' ministry in Year B, a suitable outline address is the one for the Second Sunday of Epiphany (address 1). In Year C, Jesus answers the Sadducees, who had come to him with a stupid question designed to prove their belief that there was no such thing as resurrection.

Hymns

TRADITIONAL

- *I know that my Redeemer lives*
- *Jesus calls us: o'er the tumult*
- *Now is eternal life*
- *The Lord will come and not be slow*
- *Wake, O wake! with tidings thrilling*

MODERN

- *Give me joy in my heart*
- *He is Lord*
- *I, the Lord of sea and sky*
- *James and Andrew, Peter and John*
- *Will you come and follow me*

Readings

Year A   Wisdom of Solomon 6:12-16 or Amos 5:18-24; 1 Thessalonians 4:13-18; Matthew 25:1-13

Year B   Jonah 3:1-5, 10; Hebrews 9:24-28; Mark 1:14-20

Year C   Job 19:23-27a; 2 Thessalonians 2:1-5, 13-17; Luke 20:27-38

Confession

Lord God,
we confess before you and one another
that we have sinned both in doing wrong
and in failing to do what we know is right.
We have disregarded the cry of the poor
and left the needy without justice or hope;
our worship has been
concerned with appearance
rather than obedience.
Have mercy on us,
forgive our hypocrisy and lack of care,
and fill our hearts with a new commitment
to your compassion and righteousness,
as we see them in Jesus Christ our Lord. Amen.

Absolution

Almighty God, whose promise
is that all who seek him will live,
have mercy on you,
forgive all your sins of action and neglect,
and fill you with his Spirit of justice and love,
that you may serve him faithfully
and worship him joyfully
for the sake of his Son,
our Saviour Jesus Christ. Amen.

Intercession

God of glory,
we pray that your justice and peace
may rule the Church, the world and our lives,
as we say,
Glorious Lord, may your kingdom come,
your will be done here on earth.

We pray for the world,
full of injustice and oppression;
for lives diminished by materialism and greed;
for street children and homeless teenagers;
for victims of violence or conflict;
for those sidelined by society
through no fault of their own.
Bless all peacemakers and aid-workers,
and guide those who hold the reins of power
to act justly for the good of all.
Glorious Lord, may your kingdom come,
your will be done here on earth.

We pray for the Church, throughout the world;
for Christians in an environment
of threat and persecution,
or faced with corruption and wickedness;
whose faith is tested by opposition and fear,
or who are tempted to follow the easy path
that leads to destruction.
Bless your people
as they proclaim the good news of Jesus
and show your love to a needy world.
Glorious Lord, may your kingdom come,
your will be done here on earth.

We pray for those we know
in difficult or stressful situations;
for any without jobs or livelihood;
for any without home or friends;
for any without health or strength;
for any without hope or joy in life;
especially . . .
Bless and heal them
that they may put their trust in you
and know your peace within.
Glorious Lord, may your kingdom come,
your will be done here on earth,
in us and through us,
to bring glory to Jesus Christ our Lord.
Amen.

All-age address

Jesus' parable of the ten bridesmaids is one of his best-known, but the challenge of its message is easily diluted by assumptions about its meaning. Matthew incorporates it into Jesus' teaching about the end of the age and precedes it with a parable about a faithful servant, while the conclusion makes it clear that a major part of being ready is 'keeping watch'. The two groups of bridesmaids are contrasted, but the distinction is between the foolish and the wise, the foolish being excluded from the feast because they'd not prepared themselves adequately, rather than by doing anything wrong – it can't have occurred to them that they might miss out. In this context Jesus is warning his hearers not to be complacent or unaware, because his coming will take every-one by surprise. This outline addresses the need for all Christians to be alert and ready.

1) *We must be ready for God's call.* If you have a member of the congregation who works for the emergency services, ask them to wear their uniform or bring in some equipment. Alternatively, use a large drawing or poster. A doctor or nurse must be ready to handle a medical emergency; a firefighter has to jump to action as soon as the call comes. They don't know when they might receive a call, so if they're not alert and fully prepared they can't do their job properly. Christians must be ready to obey God's call whenever it comes.

2) *We must be ready for work.* Any willing employee – a mechanic, a sales representative or a secretary, for example –could help with this by explaining their role and duties, ideally with a demonstration. To perform any task well we need the correct gear, set up to use. The bridesmaids all had the same duties, but five hadn't bargained on a long delay. They'd failed to think ahead so they had no light, and had to go off to buy more oil. Meanwhile, the bridegroom arrived, and the bridesmaids returned too late to be of any use. Prayer, Bible reading and meditation are all ways to make sure our light is still burning when Jesus returns, but they must also be translated into practical Christian service.

3) *We must be ready for what comes next.* Finish by saying that when Jesus returns in glory it will be a great celebration for those who love and serve him. If we spend all our time thinking about this world we won't be ready for the next one! God wants us to think ahead like the five wise bridesmaids, and recognise that this life is only the waiting period until the celebration starts. We don't know when that will happen, so it's up to us to be ready, and not taken by surprise.

Second Sunday before Advent

Sunday between 13th and 19th November inclusive

Our journey through each of the Gospels comes to an end next Sunday, the Festival of Christ the King, which is included in *Come to the Feast* Book 1. This Sunday, the last in Ordinary Time to be included in this volume, we reach, in Year A, the famous parable of the talents, and in Years B and C, Jesus' warnings about the future, for which you can use All-age Address 1 from the Fourth Sunday before Advent. These readings, along with those for Christ the King, prepare us for the themes of the Advent season.

Hymns

TRADITIONAL

- *Christ, whose glory fills the skies*
- *Fill thou my life, O Lord my God*
- *Judge eternal, throned in splendour*
- *Take my life, and let it be*
- *Teach me, my God and King*

MODERN

- *Heaven shall not wait*
- *Let us talents and tongues employ*
- *Seek ye first the kingdom of God*
- *Sing to God new songs of worship*
- *Within our darkest night*

Readings

Year A Zephaniah 1:7, 12-18;
1 Thessalonians 5:1-11;
Matthew 25:14-30
Year B Daniel 12:1-3; Hebrews 10:11-14
(15-18) 19-25; Mark 13:1-8
Year C Malachi 4:1-2a; 2 Thessalonians 3:6-13;
Luke 21:5-19

Confession

We confess to the Lord
the sin that so easily entangles us, saying,
In your great mercy,
Lord, forgive us.

Lord Jesus,
we repent of our faithlessness and doubt,
and ask you to help our unbelief.
In your great mercy,
Lord, forgive us.

Lord Jesus,
we repent of our self-will and pride,
and ask you to deal with our arrogance.
In your great mercy,
Lord, forgive us.

Lord Jesus, we repent of our stubbornness
and refusal to change,
and ask you to heal our insecurity.
In your great mercy,
Lord, forgive us.

Lord Jesus, we repent of all that hinders us
from following you in faith.
In your great mercy,
**Lord, forgive us,
and make us loyal and trustworthy servants
of your kingdom,
through Jesus Christ our Lord. Amen.**

Absolution

Almighty God, who is both just and forgiving,
have mercy on you,
forgive you for the wrong you have committed
and the good you have failed to do,
and give you strength to serve him
faithfully and boldly
until you see him face to face,
through our Lord and Saviour Jesus Christ.
Amen.

Intercession

We stand in the presence of Christ our Master,
bringing our requests and concerns,
and seeking his help in serving him faithfully.
Lord, receive our prayers,
and increase our faith.

We ask for your help
in being responsible members of your Church.
Give us joy in serving your purposes;
give us faith to trust your leading;
give us boldness to take your good news

to those who have not heard it;
give us courage to persevere
in the face of apathy and discouragement.
Lord, receive our prayers,
and increase our faith.

We ask for your help
in being responsible citizens
of the world and our local community.
Give us strength to uphold your kingdom;
give us wisdom to act for the good of all people;
give us confidence to challenge
evil and dishonesty.
Lord, receive our prayers,
and increase our faith.

We ask for your help
in showing compassion and care to the needy.
We pray in particular for . . .
Give healing to the sick in body or mind;
give peace to the troubled and anxious;
give hope to the depressed and despairing.
Lord, receive our prayers,
and increase our faith.

We ask for your help in serving you faithfully.
Fill us with your Spirit,
that we may be equipped with your gifts
and protected by the armour of faith.
Lord, receive our prayers,
and increase our faith,
until the day when we hear you say,
'Well done',
and enjoy for ever the presence
of our Saviour, Jesus Christ. Amen.

All-age address

Jesus' parable of the talents may seem like a gift to the British mentality of 'trying one's best', but unfortunately that's not what Jesus was referring to. Nor was he talking about our natural gifts and abilities, though these can, of course, be used for his kingdom. The talent was originally a weight, but over time it had come to mean a year's wages, and Jesus' hearers would certainly have understood him to be implying that the servants had been given considerable responsibility. However, what counts in this parable isn't the amount given to each but what they'd done with it. The

religious leaders were again the target because they'd failed to fulfil their responsibilities as guardians of the law. They'd preserved it unchanged, and unspoiled by ordinary people, but, in so doing, had turned Israel from being a faith community into a quagmire of religious and legal red tape. They couldn't handle a relationship with God over which they had no control, so they refused to countenance any changes to the status quo. They'd misunderstood totally what God was like and, like the third servant, tried to use this as an excuse. Today's Church would do well to look to itself before condemning that servant! This outline aims to highlight some unhelpful views of God, and then to illustrate how faith demands that we take risks. Preparation involves a trip to the dressing-up box, or some simple drawing.

1) Find a police helmet and truncheon, and dress a volunteer in them (alternatively, show an OHP slide of a very stern-looking police officer). Ask the congregation what comes to mind. Likely answers include getting into trouble, being arrested, or being handcuffed. Point out that many people (including some Christians) see God in the same way, a stern figure who watches our every move, noting down each misdemeanour to use in evidence against us, always on the lookout for faults to incriminate us with.

2) Next find a wig and red cloak, and maybe a gavel, so that someone can be dressed up as a judge (or show a picture of an angry judge wagging his finger). If you ask how people view a judge, you're likely to get answers like being sent to prison, being told off, being condemned. Again, explain that many people see God as an angry judge who can't wait to prove that we've done wrong and punish us. God is certainly our judge, but he longs to set us free rather than imprison, and to forgive instead of condemn.

3) The third dressing-up costume is for Santa Claus (a picture would be a simple alternative). This time the general opinion will be that he's benevolent and kind, turns a blind eye to our faults, and hands out

presents to everyone. This is the opposite view of God, seeing him as a kindly uncle figure who makes no demands and showers us with gifts.

4) For the second part of the address you'll need a packet of small seeds and a sample of the plant they will grow into. A small pot of compost is also needed. Take a handful of seed and ask someone to identify it (seed can appear to be dust). The only way to prove whether or not you're telling the truth is to plant them and see what happens. When they've been placed in the pot, leave them for a few seconds, then look again and complain that they're not growing. Eventually the seeds will grow into beautiful plants, but patience and time are needed before this happens. God gives us the seeds of faith, but it's our responsibility to nurture them. If we don't open the packet it will still look intact and beautiful on the outside, but there's no chance of any plants growing. For that to happen we have to open the packet, sow the seeds in suitable soil, and let them grow. It involves a certain amount of risk, but the end result makes it worthwhile. Likewise, if we don't use our faith, take a few risks for God, and give it a chance to grow, our lives will never bear fruit for God's kingdom. If we offer God our faith, however small it may seem, and move forwards trusting his guidance, it will grow like the seed, into something infinitely greater.

BIBLE SUNDAY

The last Sunday after Trinity falls on the last Sunday of October (or 24th October if 31st October is a Sunday and kept as All Saints' Day). The collect is adapted from the one in the Book of Common Prayer for the Second Sunday of Advent, a day often known as 'Bible Sunday', but it was decided to relocate Bible Sunday to tie in with what some denominations call 'Reformation Sunday', and to provide a three-year cycle of readings for those churches wishing to keep it. All three Gospel readings deal with God's word and our belief: in Year A, Jesus reassures his disciples that his words will never pass away; in Year B, he accuses the Jews of refusing to believe that the Scriptures bear witness to him; and in Year C, we have Luke's well-known account of Jesus preaching in the synagogue in Nazareth.

Hymns

TRADITIONAL

- *Firmly I believe and truly*
- *Hail to the Lord's anointed*
- *Hark, the glad sound*
- *Lord, thy word abideth*
- *O for a thousand tongues to sing*

MODERN

- *As the deer pants for the water*
- *God's Spirit is in my heart*
- *Make way, make way*
- *Open our eyes, Lord*
- *You are the King of Glory*

Readings

Year A   Nehemiah 8:1-4a (5-6) 8-12; Colossians 3:12-17; Matthew 24:30-35

Year B   Isaiah 55:1-11; 2 Timothy 3:14-4:5; John 5:36b-47

Year C   Isaiah 45:22-25; Romans 15:1-6; Luke 4:16-24

Confession

Lord, you have given us your word to guide;
we are sorry for going our own way.
You have given us your word to instruct;
we are sorry for not learning of you.
You have given us your word
to reveal your love and grace;
we are sorry for turning our backs on you.
Have mercy on us,
and forgive all our sins;
open our hearts
to receive your word with gladness,
and make us worthy ambassadors
of your kingdom,
for the sake of our Saviour, Jesus Christ.
Amen.

Absolution

Almighty God, whose word brings life and joy,
have mercy on you,
pardon all your wrongdoing,
and deliver you from the death of sin
into the new life to be found only
in your living Word, Jesus Christ our Lord.
Amen.

Intercession

We approach the throne of the Lord our God,
bringing our prayers and burdens,
and waiting for him to speak to us.
Lord, we praise you for your word,
and wait on you in faith.

Speak to your Church, Lord,
words of encouragement and challenge,
as it fulfils your great commission
to bring the Gospel to all the world.
Release the gifts of the Spirit in your people,
that teachers and leaders,
evangelists and mission workers,
pastors and carers
may bring your love to those
who do not know you.
Lord, we praise you for your word,
and wait on you in faith.

Speak to those in authority, Lord,
words of wisdom and guidance,

as they confront wickedness and violence,
poverty and starvation,
degradation and exploitation.
Influence their decisions and direction
that they may uphold the justice
and righteousness of your kingdom.
Lord, we praise you for your word,
and wait on you in faith.

Speak to those in distress or despair, Lord,
words of comfort and healing,
that in their suffering they may know
the touch of your hand.
We remember especially . . .
Bring them relief from their pain and distress,
wholeness of body and mind,
and the unfading hope of eternal glory.
Lord, we praise you for your word,
and wait on you in faith.

Speak to those who mourn
the loss of loved ones, Lord,
words of peace,
that in their grief
they may know you beside them.
We remember especially . . .
May we be uplifted by the example
of those who have died in faith,
and follow after them
 in the way of truth and light that leads to you.
Lord, we praise you for your word,
and wait on you in faith,
trusting in your mercy and obeying your call,
until we reach our home in heaven,
for Christ's sake. Amen.

All-age address

The passage from Luke 4 is covered by the outline address for the Third Sunday of Epiphany, while the Second Sunday of Advent (found in Book 1) has two addresses suitable for Bible Sunday. As an alternative, this simple outline uses the concept of a library to illustrate the varied types of literature contained in the Bible, and the ways in which we can use it. It's equally important to point out that there are unhelpful ways of reading Scripture too, such as taking short phrases out of their context or using 'proof texts' to justify personal opinions or behaviour. You could add to the impact by putting your chosen books on a small bookshelf.

1) Start off by displaying a couple of history books from your collection – perhaps a glossy, illustrated coffee-table volume and something that looks a bit more erudite. Ask the congregation why we read about events of the past and people who have died. Several reasons may emerge – for example, to learn from their examples or mistakes; to remember milestones in the history of a community or nation; to learn about the history and culture of other peoples; to interpret facts about the past for our own times. The Bible contains history for all these reasons, but with one addition – to recall the saving acts of God in the history of his people, supremely in the person of his Son, Jesus Christ.

2) Next move on to biography, using an example or two. History is made by people, and most of us are fascinated by the lives of the history-makers whose names live on after their death. We may be inspired by their example and achievements, motivated by their commitment and enthusiasm, or warned by their mistakes. The Bible also focuses on people, but not just biographically. It leaves out some of the small details we like to know (for example, what Jesus looked like), and concentrates instead on their relationship with God, and the part they played in his plans.

3) We all like a good novel, either for its depiction of characters or its gripping plot – you could ask for some congregational favourites at this point before revealing your own! However, a good novel does more than entertain; it seeks to present a perspective on human life and enable the reader to see a situation in a particular light. The four Gospels and the Acts of the Apostles certainly make for good reading, but they describe real people and events rather than using invented situations. The books of Job and Jonah are good examples of writing aimed specifically at helping the reader understand or come to terms with the problem of suffering.

4) Poetry may seem a more esoteric kind of reading-matter (again tastes may be sampled

from the congregation), but there's plenty of it in the Bible. It was a normal way of expressing the whole range of human emotions, and, while the Psalms are the most obvious example, the prophets often expressed their message in poetic form too, maybe as an aid to memory. Some of the most profound parts of the Bible are expressed in its poetic sections – Handel made good use of some in his oratorio *Messiah*.

5) Collections of letters written by the famous are also popular, shedding light on their character and feelings. Much of the New Testament is taken up with letters, but while they reveal something about their writers, they were written to some of the earliest churches to be read aloud at meetings; those included in the Bible were considered to be important for all Christians in all generations and cultures.

6) Books are also published to promote and spread the views of their authors – Hitler's *Mein Kampf* is a modern example of this. The prophets weren't afraid of saying what they thought, but they knew this was a message from God for his people. The books in the Bible weren't written to popularise an individual, but to ensure that God's word reached those he wanted to hear it.

Conclude by emphasising that the Bible consists of a wide range of books – and we can learn from all of them, not just about a nation's history, nor even just about the words and deeds of a few inspiring people, but most of all about our heavenly Father, who through his written word leads us to his Son Jesus, the living Word.

DEDICATION FESTIVAL

The Dedication Festival is not to be confused with the Patronal Festival. It provides an opportunity once a year to give thanks for the bricks and mortar of the church building and its role in the local community. A church in a newer building will be aware of the date of its dedication or consecration to God, and would celebrate this festival on or near that date. Most ancient buildings, however, have no records of this, so the new lectionary suggests that it's kept on either the first or the last Sunday of October. It would be wrong to become fixated on buildings, and there's a general agreement that the Church consists of dedicated people rather than building materials, but an annual thanksgiving for a 'holy place' may also give the opportunity to review how it might be used for the benefit of the people who worship there, (and those who don't). The Gospel readings for Years A and C both concern Jesus' cleansing of the Temple, while Year B's is the conclusion of the Good Shepherd discourse.

Hymns

TRADITIONAL

- *Angel-voices ever singing*
- *Christ is made the sure foundation*
- *Christ is our cornerstone*
- *City of God, how broad and far*
- *We love the place, O God*

MODERN

- *As we are gathered*
- *For I'm building a people of power*
- *Give me joy in my heart*
- *I will enter his gates*
- *Lord, for the years*

Readings

Year A   1 Kings 8:22-30 or Revelation 21:9-14;
          Hebrews 12:18-24; Matthew 21:12-16
Year B   Genesis 28:11-18 or Revelation 21:9-14;
          1 Peter 2:1-10; John 10:22-29
Year C   1 Chronicles 29:6-19; Ephesians 2:19-22;
          John 2:13-22

Confession

Most merciful God, our loving Father,
you call us to be the Body of Christ
here on earth.
We confess that we have sinned
against you and one another
in what we have said and done,
and have failed to do.
We have harboured unfair thoughts
and unjust attitudes;
we have uttered rude and insensitive words;
we have acted selfishly and irresponsibly.
Have mercy on us
and forgive all our sins, we pray;
help us not to countenance evil
but to celebrate goodness and truth,
for the building up of your people
in the love of your Son, Jesus Christ our Lord.
Amen.

Absolution

Almighty God, whose mercy never fails
but endures for ever,
grant you pardon for all your sin,
deliverance from temptation,
and the peace
which binds us together in his love,
for the sake of his Son,
our Saviour Jesus Christ. Amen.

Intercession

We bring to God our thanksgiving and praise
for his goodness in the past
and offer him our prayers,
our gifts and our service, saying,
Lord, we rejoice in your goodness;
accept the offering of our praise.

We thank you for the blessings
you have showered
on your people over the years:
for faithful ministry, loyal service
and generous provision.
Grant us wisdom to use our resources wisely,
to encourage one another in the life of faith,
and to work together in fulfilling

your great commission to make disciples.
Lord, we rejoice in your goodness;
accept the offering of our praise.

We thank you for the gifts and strength
with which you have equipped your people:
gifts of leadership,
evangelism, teaching and healing.
Grant us discernment to use our abilities
and gifts to build up the whole Church
in faith and unity,
and to bring your care and mercy
to our needy world.
Lord, we rejoice in your goodness;
accept the offering of our praise.

We thank you for the prayers
you have answered,
and the times when you have heard
your people's cry:
in times of crisis and anxiety,
of illness and misery,
of anguish and grief.
We name before you now . . .
Grant us compassion to come alongside them
in this time of darkness,
and bring them the light of your presence.
Lord, we rejoice in your goodness;
accept the offering of our praise.

We thank you for those
who have served you faithfully and well,
and now rest in you,
having completed their earthly pilgrimage,
especially . . .
Grant us faith to follow in their footsteps
and finish our journey,
that we may one day share with them
the joys of eternal life.
Lord, we rejoice in your goodness;
**accept the offering of our lives,
for the sake of your Son,
our Saviour Jesus Christ. Amen.**

All-age address

Many Christians, especially church leaders,
feel ambivalent about their church buildings.
There's good biblical precedent for setting
aside a hallowed space, dedicated to the
worship of God, but it can seem out of all
proportion to the often small number of people
using it. Many churches are attractive, even
beautiful, yet their maintenance can be costly,
absorbing money which might otherwise be
used to help the needy. Ancient buildings, in
particular, take up an inordinate amount of
time which might otherwise be devoted to
mission and evangelism. Some will even point
out that St Paul and the earliest Church had no
buildings set apart for their use – in fact, the
world's earliest surviving Christian building
(in Syria) is a converted dwelling, dating only
from the third century. True, the Church is made
up of people rather than bricks and mortar, but
buildings do reflect the life of those who use
them, and for many regular church-goers their
premises feel like a second home. There's good
reason to give thanks for a church building,
and the celebrations may provide an excellent
opportunity to draw in other members of
the local community. This outline aims to
demonstrate how a church building is just an
empty shell unless it's also built up with God's
people. It requires some preparation, and the
involvement not just of key church officers but
also of the whole congregation. You'll need an
outline drawing, as large as possible, of a
church building (ideally your own), together
with a brick-sized piece of paper for as many
members of the congregation as you think
feasible, including some who hold positions of
responsibility.

1) The drawing of the church should be
displayed prominently on a wall, an easel,
or any other convenient surface. Start by
asking what different parts there are to
the church, and as you get answers, ask
someone connected with each part to come
forward and place a 'brick' on the picture on
which they write what they do. The organ
is represented by the organist, the sanctuary
by the chief sacristan, the guttering by the
churchwarden and so on. Explain that while
the building may be beautiful or functional
(rarely both!), it won't be much use if there
aren't any people using it. God gives each
of us gifts and wants us to use them for the
benefit of the whole church. Practical people
can use their gift to keep the building in
sound and safe condition; artistic people
can make it look beautiful; musical people

can fill it with God's praise; friendly people can make it a place of encouragement and fellowship; those with a pastoral gift can make it a place where people feel cared for. This can be developed as much as time allows.

2) Now invite the rest of the congregation to write on their piece of paper what part they think God wants them to play in his building. When this is done, each of them comes and attaches their 'brick' to an appropriate part of the drawing. Finally, when all are seated again, say that while we thank God for our buildings, all Christians are called to be built together so that the church isn't a dead shell but a living fellowship.